Vicky McClure is a hugely talented and much-loved actress known for playing DI Kate Fleming in *Line of Duty* (the most watched BBC drama since records began), Lana Washington in *Trigger Point* and Lol in *This is England*. She is also the founder of *Our Dementia Choir*, which compassionately explores the impact of music therapy on those living with dementia. She is passionate about demystifying the disease for the younger generation.

@vicky.mcclure

@Vicky_McClure

Published in the UK by Scholastic, 2023
1 London Bridge, London, SE1 9BG
Scholastic Ireland, 89E Lagan Road, Dublin Industrial Estate,
Glasnevin, Dublin, D11 HP5F

Text © Vicky McClure, 2023
Illustrations by Alan Brown © Scholastic, 2023

ISBN 978 0702 32402 4

A CIP catalogue record for this book
is available from the British Library.

Printed by CPI Group (UK) Ltd, Croydon, CR0 4YY
Papers used by Scholastic Children's Books are made
from wood grown in sustainable forests.

1 3 5 7 9 10 8 6 4 2

www.scholastic.co.uk

VICKY McCLURE

IN COLLABORATION WITH KIM CURRAN

CASTLE ROCK MYSTERY CREW

THE JASE FILES

■SCHOLASTIC

Friends become family, and family
is a feeling that can never be forgotten.

Dedicated to Tyrone. Love and Peace x

This was it. The thrill of the chase. Jase had spent days staring at clues, piecing bits of the puzzle together, thinking until his head ached. But now he had the thief in his sights, and he wasn't going to let them get away. His heart pounded, his muscles ached, and yet he'd never felt more alive. This was what being a detective was about.

He had grown up on his nana's stories of solving crimes and chasing down criminals. And at last, he had solved a case of his own.

Just a few more steps and it would be over. Just a few more steps and...

"Wait!"

He stopped and turned slowly around. He'd come so far. He couldn't turn back now. No matter what it took, he was going to catch his thief.

CHAPTER ONE

It was 3:13 on a Friday. Two minutes until the end of the day. Two minutes until the end of the school year. And you could practically *smell* the anticipation in the air. Even over the whiff of sulphuric acid from Miss Clarke's chemistry experiment.

Everyone was *buzzing* for the summer holidays to start. Everyone except Jase.

Oh, he wanted school to end – especially this boring chemistry lesson. (Miss Clarke had promised it would end the year with a BANG, but something had gone wrong and the chemicals had only fizzed.) But he wasn't as excited about the summer break as the rest of his friends. They would all be off on exotic holidays abroad while he would be staying at home with his mum and helping look after Nana Rose.

At last, the school bell rang. There was an explosion of cheering as the class all jumped to their feet.

"One minute!" Miss Clarke shouted over the excited chattering. "Before you all race off on your holidays, it's Jase's tenth birthday tomorrow. And as is class tradition…" Miss Clarke waved her hands around and conducted the class in an out-of-tune, out-of-time rendition of "Happy Birthday to You".

Jase went bright red. He wished the floor would open up and swallow him whole.

When the cringe was finally over, Miss Clarke wished them all a good summer.

Jase grabbed his bag and followed his classmates out. He narrowly missed bumping into a Year Six boy charging down the corridor.

"FREEEEDOOOOOM!" the boy screamed, a trail of shredded paper in his wake. Ripping up your classwork and scribbling on each other's shirts were end-of-year traditions for Year Six.

Jase jumped when his friend Carl slapped him on the back.

"Jase! My man! What you doing this summer?"

"Not much," Jase said. "You?"

"Disneyland, baby!" Carl said, holding his hand up for a high five.

Jase hit Carl's hand without much enthusiasm. "Have fun!"

"You too, bro. You too!" Carl vanished through the school doors.

Jase waved goodbye to his other friends and headed for home.

He turned left out of the black school gates, dodging scooters and footballs and frantic parents picking up their kids. He passed Mr Nash, their headteacher, who sometimes took them for PE. He had a bald head and red cheeks and wheezed when refereeing football matches.

"Have a great break, Jase!" he said, giving an energetic thumbs up. "And don't forget to keep up your reading."

"Will do, Mr Nash," Jase said with a weak smile.

He wasn't going to tell him that the only reading he planned on doing this summer was comic books and true crime stories. Hardly school curriculum stuff.

It wasn't that Jase didn't like school. He liked seeing his friends and playing kick-about at break. And he liked English and history — especially learning about the gruesome stuff people used to do to each other in the past. But he couldn't see how most of the stuff he learned would be of any use when he grew up and joined the police force. Like, when would he need to know about chemical reactions when he was bringing criminals to justice? Unless one of them was cooking up a chemical bomb and he needed to know how to defuse it! Maybe he should have paid attention to Miss Clarke after all? The fate of the world might depend on it!

He daydreamed about solving crimes and catching bad guys a lot. He'd make up wild theories about what the people on his estate were really up to. Once, he got into trouble sneaking out at the crack of dawn because he wanted to stake out the mums who went jogging in the morning. (He had been sure they were part of a burglary crime ring. They weren't.)

His mum said he watched too much TV. But he mostly got it from his nana. He'd grown up listening to her thrilling stories about her time as a detective in the Nottinghamshire Police. Even now, when she was starting to forget everything else, she could remember every detail of her life on the beat. Jase wanted to be just like her when he grew up.

It normally took Jase ten minutes to walk back to Fernwood Gate estate. Today, it took him nearly half an hour. He looked in shop windows. Stopped to pat a dog. He wanted to drag out this time a little longer. The space between the end of school and the long six-week break. Six weeks with nothing to do and no friends to do it with.

He walked under the graffiti-covered underpass and across the grass field, which had gone all yellow and brittle in the heat. There was no one around. Even the rusting playground, which was usually swarming with kids climbing up the frames and trying to see who could swing the highest, was empty.

He felt like he was in one of those zombie movies and he was the last boy alive.

Jase dragged himself up the four flights of concrete stairs to his flat.

He pulled the key from around his neck and let himself in.

Sherlock came bounding down the hallway, his floppy beagle ears flapping and his stubby tail wagging.

"Ay up, mate," Jase said, giving the dog a scratch behind his floppy ears.

Sherlock barked twice to confirm that he was indeed a good boy.

The sound of laughter floated down the hallway from the kitchen. It wasn't his mum's or his nana's laugh.

Someone else was there.

CHAPTER TWO

"Auntie Nicki!" Jase said, when he saw who was sitting at the kitchen table with his mum and nana. He ran over and gave his auntie a hug.

Nicki had short dark hair and bright green eyes which always twinkled like she was up to no good. She was still dressed in her pink nurse's scrubs and smelled a bit of disinfectant from the hospital. She was his favourite of his mum's two sisters. She brought him the best gifts and when she was left in charge – which wasn't as often as he liked – there were no rules. It was all water fights and no bedtimes. Sometimes, she acted more like a kid than Jase did. Like the time she built a fort out of the settee cushions and made everyone

guess a password before they could come in. Or when she stuck googly eyes on the vegetables and acted out a puppet show with them. She was always making faces and putting on voices. Jase loved her.

"Here he is," she said, ruffling his hair.

"Good day at school, babe?" his mum asked.

"Yeah, a'rite. Glad it's over." He gave his mum a quick kiss too and then turned to his nana.

"Hey, Nana ... Ruby? Poppy? Something flowery." He clicked his fingers. "Rose! Nana Rose!"

Nana Rose laughed and pinched his cheek. "You cheeky pup, you."

This was a silly game they played. His nana had dementia. When she was first diagnosed, she would get really upset that she was losing her memory. So, Jase would pretend to forget things too. Making a big fuss out of forgetting stuff like what a fork was called or what his own name was. Until his nana started laughing.

It wasn't always that easy, though. She would have good days when she was just like her old self. Telling her gripping – sometimes gory – stories about being a police detective. And then she'd have bad days, when the sparkle in her eyes would dull and it was like living with a different person. Nana Rose had moved in with them a year ago. His mum had given up her job in the supermarket to look after her full-time. Jase had given up his bedroom and now shared with his older brother, Ross. But he didn't mind. Good days or bad, he liked having Nana Rose around. No one was as interesting as her.

He pulled up a chair at the kitchen table and grabbed some biscuits off a plate in the middle. He shoved two into his mouth before his mum could stop him.

"You'll ruin your dinner."

"*Vank ooo,*" he said, spitting cookie crumbs over the table.

When he'd swallowed the biscuits, he turned to his auntie. "What are you doing here?"

"How's that for a welcome?" Nicki said, pretending to sound offended.

"I didn't mean it like that," Jase said, sticking his tongue out at her.

She stuck hers out back.

"Nicki has a bit of a surprise for you, Jase."

A surprise? Jase's brain whirred, wondering what it could be. Tickets to Alton Towers? A shopping trip? Match tickets? Or maybe the surprise was about her? Maybe she was getting married? Not that Jase knew of Nicki having a partner. She always said she was too busy having fun to settle down.

"How do you fancy coming on holiday with me and your nana?" Nicki asked.

"Holiday!" Jase said. "Where?"

He immediately pictured himself lazing on a lounger on a white-sandy beach, sipping a cold drink from a coconut.

"Castle Rock Caravan Park in Skegness!" Nicki said.

The image of the sandy beach and coconut drink vanished in a poof!

"It's where Mum used to take us when we were little," Nicki continued. "And it's not far."

"Skeggy," Nana Rose said with a wistful sigh. "Best place on the planet."

Well, it might not be an exotic beach holiday, but that didn't sound too bad, Jase thought.

"And we'll all be going?" Jase asked, excited. They hadn't had a family holiday in years.

"It would just be you, Auntie Nicki and your nana," his mum said. There was a crease above her nose, so Jase knew she was worried. "Your brothers are going to stay here. Mark and Will have summer jobs, and Ross has been working so hard on his exams he says he just wants to sleep all summer."

"Oh," Jase said. He'd thought it would be all of them having a holiday together. He'd never been away without his mum.

"We'll have the best time, Jase, I promise," Nicki said. "Ten whole days of fun. You can eat ice cream till you're sick and no boring Mum around to tell you when to wash behind your ears!" She reached across the table and pulled at his earlobe.

He laughed and pushed her away. "Geroff."

"Besides," Nana said, "your mum needs a break from looking after this old bag!" She pointed to herself.

"Mum! It's not that..." Jase's mum started to say.

His nana waved her objection away with a wrinkled hand. "Oh, come on now. I know me and my dementia are a pain in your backside, Penny!"

His nana wasn't wrong. Jase knew that looking after Nana Rose was hard for his mum. He sometimes caught her crying when she thought no one was looking. So, Nicki taking Nana Rose away for a week would be just the break his mum needed. But why did *he* have to go with them?

Jase felt a stab of jealousy towards his three older brothers, who would get to stay home and do whatever they wanted. He was only nine. Ten in less than twelve hours. But as much as he liked to think he was a grown-up, he knew he still needed taking care of.

Maybe his mum needed some time when the only person she had to take care of was herself?

"You don't have to go if you don't want to, love," his mum said.

Jase looked at the three women sat around the table. They all had the same bright green eyes that seemed able to look into your thoughts. They were waiting to see what he would decide.

Maybe it'll be fun? Jase thought. He'd never been to a caravan park. And it had to be better than sitting around the flat doing nothing all summer.

"Yeah!" he said, trying to sound as happy as he could. "Sounds great!"

Nicki whooped and Nana clapped. His mum gave

his hand a gentle squeeze and mouthed, *"Thank you."*

"Then you'd better go pack your swimming shorts, Jasey boy," Nicki said. "We're leaving first thing in the morning!"

CHAPTER THREE

They set off early to avoid the Saturday morning traffic and arrived in Skegness in under two hours. Nicki said that was a record.

"Yeah, a *criminal* record," Nana Rose said. "You were speeding."

"I was not," Nicki snapped back. "Besides, you're not a copper any more, Mum."

"I'm not? Oh." Nana was having one of her not so good days. She was struggling to remember even simple things.

"You OK, Nana?" Jase asked, catching her eye in the mirror.

"I'm fine and dandy, Jase. Don't you worry about

me." Nana Rose turned and winked at him.

He gave her a smile back. Maybe if he pretended everything was all right, it would be.

She turned to look at the road again. "Where are we going?" she asked for the fifth time.

"To the caravan, Mum," Nicki said gently.

"Oh yes, I keep forgetting. But what do you expect? I have dementia!" She laughed, trying to make a joke out of it. But Jase could tell by the wobble in her voice that she was finding it all a bit stressful.

He was sitting quietly in the back playing with the phone he'd got for his birthday. It had belonged to one of his older brothers, but now it was his. His very first phone!

"So you can call me every night and give me an update on all the fun you're having!" his mum had said.

Jase had given her the biggest hug. Most of his friends had phones already. He quickly found as many of them as he could on Snapchat and fired off messages.

You got a phone! Welcome to the twenty-first century, Carl replied. Followed by a picture of an airport lounge. **Delayed flight to Paris. Been here for DAAAAAAYYS!**

At least Jase didn't have that to worry about. They were nearly at the site.

Sherlock had stuck his head out of the window the whole way, tongue and ears flapping in the wind. He looked put out when the car slowed down for the speed bumps leading to the gate.

"Here we are!" Nicki said.

A large blue sign read: WELCOME TO CASTLE ROCK CARAVAN PARK OF SKEGNESS. It had three yellow stars across the top, which were peeling a little.

They waited for the security barrier to lift and drove on to the site.

Jase put his phone down so he could take it all in. There were winding roads heading out in all directions with row after row of caravans parked up like neat LEGO bricks. Every caravan was different. Some had blooming flowers surrounding them, with pink flamingos and garden gnomes (he saw one gnome pulling a moony!). Some people had decorated their caravans with fairy lights and bunting, while others had painted theirs bright ice-cream colours. Everywhere he looked, Jase saw flags waving in the breeze. All different nationalities, football teams, rainbow flags, even pirate flags!

Adults lazed on loungers on the raised decking while screaming kids ran in and out of the caravans, chasing each other with water pistols. Other kids *zoomed* past on electric scooters or pulled wheelies on bikes.

It was an explosion of colour and noise and … the smell! The whole place smelled of BBQ. Jase's mouth started to water.

A young girl carrying a cuddly toy waved to him and he waved back.

"The clubhouse is down there," Nicki said, pointing out the left car window. "And that's the arcade." They drove past a building on the right with GOLD COAST ARCADE written on it in bright neon lights. Through the window, Jase could see the flashing lights of games machines.

"It has its own arcade?" Jase said in wonder. He'd

been imagining rusty old caravans and, if he was lucky, a mini golf course. Nothing like this.

"Of course. And we're only a twenty-minute walk to Fantasy Island Theme Park."

Jase had been reading about Fantasy Island on the way down. It was the biggest amusement park on the east coast. The rides had names like The Volcano and Turbulence. He'd never even *been* on a roller coaster.

Nicki stopped the car to let an old woman cross the road. She looked older than his nana. In her late eighties maybe. She had bright purple hair, a tatty red handbag and bright pink lipstick. She was the first person he'd seen so far who wasn't smiling. She stared at Nana through the car window, her puckered mouth opening and closing as if she was trying to think of something to say. When nothing came to her, she turned away and kept crossing.

"Do you know her?" Nicki asked.

"Never seen her before," Nana Rose said. "At least, I don't *think* I have." She had the uncertain quiver in her voice that gave Jase unpleasant squirming in his belly.

"She's probably just jealous of your scarf," Jase said, trying to make light of it.

"And who could blame her?" Nana Rose replied, adjusting the silk yellow scarf she wore in a bow around her neck.

When the old lady had finally made her way to the safety of the pavement, they drove on deeper into the heart of the caravan site. Jase was already wondering how he was going to find his way around. This place was like a small town!

Every corner had a sign giving directions and laying out the rules of the site. One caught Jase's attention.

"No BB guns," he said, reading the sign out loud. "What's a BB gun?"

He hadn't thought there would be *guns* here. The closest Jase had got to a gun was when he went paintballing. He'd ended up covered in bruises and with fluorescent paint on his face that wouldn't come off for days. He was suddenly worried this might be a dangerous place.

"It's an air rifle," Nicki said. "The kind you use to shoot ducks in the arcade. Don't look so worried, Jase, Castle Rock is one of the safest places in the country! Everyone leaves their doors open. Nothing bad ever happens here! Isn't that right, Mum?"

Nana Rose was deep in thought, staring out at the caravans.

"Castle Rock," she said at last. "I remember now! We came here every summer when your grandpops was still alive. Best place on the planet!" She smiled, and it was brighter than any of the neon signs.

"We're up here," Nicki said as they turned right off the main road and into a winding cul-de-sac.

They drove past three kids around Jase's age playing basketball. One boy and two girls. The hoop was attached to the side of one of the caravans. Jase turned to watch through the back car window as one of the girls scored a point. They all celebrated with a complicated handshake.

"OK," Jase said, turning back round, "this place is COOL!"

"You didn't think I was going to take you somewhere boring, did you?" Nicki said, smiling at him in the rear–view mirror.

CHAPTER FOUR

Sherlock bounded out of the car and ran straight up the steps of a caravan. It had a faded grey sign that read SANDY VIEW.

Sherlock sat on the doorstep, his tail banging on the wooden decking.

"He must remember it from when we used to come down here," Nana Rose said.

Sherlock had originally been Nana Rose's dog, but when she started struggling to look after herself, she wasn't able to take care of him. So now he belonged to Jase.

Nicki nudged Sherlock out of the way so she could unlock the door, while Jase helped Nana up the steps.

"Welcome," Nicki said, hand on the handle, "to Sandy View." She opened the door.

When Jase had heard "caravan", he'd imagined the kind of thing that cars towed behind them. Or the ones you saw rusting away by the side of the motorway. This was like a small house.

They walked into the living room. It had two brown leatherette settees and a single blue fabric armchair. There was a low coffee table in the middle with a pile of old boardgames stashed underneath. The curtains were polka-dot pink, tied back with lace ribbons. To the left was a small kitchenette, with sink and hob, and at the back were large French windows that looked out on to a large pond behind the caravans.

It smelled a bit musty, and the decor hadn't been updated since the 80s. But Jase instantly loved it.

It felt like home.

Sherlock jumped up on the armchair, circled a few times, and promptly fell asleep.

"Make yourself at home," Nicki said, giving Jase a quick hug. "I'll unpack the car."

Jase helped his nana on to the settee. A cloud of dust puffed up into the air when she sat down, and the settee made a *pffffff* sound.

"That was the settee!" she said.

Jase pretended to waft a smell away, then jumped on to the opposite settee. It made the same *pffffffft* noise. He and his nana squished and squashed around, trying to make the settees fart again.

To join in the fun, Sherlock farted in his sleep. A real fart this time.

That was it. Nana Rose and Jase fell about laughing. Neither of them could stop.

Nicki returned, dragging in their three suitcases. "What's so funny?"

It was too silly to explain.

She put the suitcases down. "You picked your room yet, Jase?"

My room? thought Jase. He hadn't had a room of his own in nearly a year. He jumped up and *raced* off to find the bedrooms.

The first bedroom had a double bed with a yellow flowery duvet cover and a picture of a big fish on the wall. Dust motes floated in the light breaking through the net curtains. The second had a single bed with a plain white duvet. Faded posters of rock musicians were pinned to the wall with purple thumb tacks. Jase would put money on this being Nicki's old bedroom. He opened the door to the third room. Light streamed through the open curtains on to a small single bed, which had a blue-and-white striped cover. There was a small table and chair in the corner. He looked out of the window. He could see the back of the caravan next door, but if he went on his tiptoes … in the distance he could see the sea! It was perfect.

Beaming, Jase walked back to the living room.

"Happy?" Nicki asked.

"Happy," he replied.

Nana Rose got off the settee with a bit of effort. She ran her fingertips over the knick-knacks on the sideboards, as if soaking up the feel of everything. A pottery frog. A model ship. A brass clock. She stopped in front of an old grey stereo. The type that took cassettes. With a shaky finger, she pressed play.

Music blasted out of the player, filling the whole caravan. Jase didn't recognize the song. But his nana did.

She sang along at the top of her voice. As it played, Jase felt as if the whole caravan was filled with light.

Nana Rose had the most beautiful voice. She used to sing him lullabies when he was little. And, in the past, it didn't take much persuading for her to get up and

give them all a song at the pub. But Jase hadn't heard her sing in ages. Her eyes were shining, and she was smiling bigger than she had in months. It was like the old Nana was back.

"It was our holiday song," Nicki said, resting a hand on Jase's shoulder. "She and Dad loved it."

Jase watched in wonder as his nana sang and swayed in time to the music. She often struggled with finding the right words when speaking, but singing along to the song, she knew every word.

"Get over here and dance with your old nana," she said, reaching her hand out.

Jase didn't know how to dance. But he took her hand, and she started swinging him around like he was a human yo-yo. Nicki joined them and they danced and sang and laughed till they couldn't breathe.

When the song ended, they collapsed on to the settee. Jase hadn't felt this happy in ages.

"Me and your grandpops used to dance to that," Nana said, her eyes sparkling. "Oh, gis me my bag, will you?"

Jase passed over her handbag. She rooted around inside it. Handkerchiefs, a pack of sweets, an umbrella, three pairs of glasses and four white bottles of pills were all poured out on to the coffee table before she found what she was after. A small square parcel wrapped up in blue paper.

"Happy birthday, ducky."

Jase took the parcel. It had been wrapped in so many

layers of Sellotape he had to rip it with his teeth.

It was a coin, the size of a 2p, with a woman on a throne on one side, and an old man with a beard on the other. It said One Penny around the top.

"Your grandpops gave that to me the day we met. He picked it up off the floor and gave it to me for luck. Said that I was the only luck he needed." Her lips tightened as she tried not to cry. His nana hated crying in front of him. "I always carried it when I went out on my police patrols. Anyways. It might be worth a bob or two now. You should look it up on that gaggle thing."

"Google, Mum," Nicki said.

"I know. Was just playing," she said with a wink.

"Thanks, Nana!" Jase said.

"I guess I should give you my gift now then?" Nicki said.

Jase had been wondering when she might remember. He hadn't wanted to sound greedy and ask.

She unzipped her suitcase and pulled out a plastic bag. In it was a white shoebox.

Jase pulled the box out. It had a blue tick painted on the side. She hadn't, had she? She had!

He opened the box to reveal a shining pair of red-and-white Jordans. Not just any Jordans. These were Air Jordan 1 Retro High OGs.

"Well, don't just gawp at them," his auntie said. "Try 'em on."

Jase kicked off his tatty old trainers and pulled on the Jordans. They fit perfectly. He stood up and bounced up and down. He felt like he was walking on air. And it wasn't just because of the cushioned soles.

"The guy in the shop said these are the ones the real sneaker-heads are after."

"I love them!" Jase bounced over and gave his auntie a hug. "The coin too, Nana." He gave her a squeeze too.

For lunch they ate the sandwiches Jase's mum had prepared and the snacks and sweets Nicki had thrown in without his mum seeing.

"Right, shall I get a brew on?" Nicki said when they'd finished eating.

"Forget that," Nana said, slapping her hands on her thighs. "I think all of this calls for a G&T at the clubhouse."

"It's only one thirty," Jase said, looking at his watch. He looked over at Nicki. She was a nurse so she would know if it was OK for Nana Rose to be drinking.

She shrugged.

"Clocks work different here," his nana said. "We're on Castle Rock time now!" She cackled.

Nicki gave her mum a hand to get up off the settee and the two women strolled out the door, arm in arm.

Jase left his birthday coin safely in a bowl on the coffee table, along with a pile of pound coins. He didn't want to risk losing it.

Besides, he already felt like the luckiest boy ever.

CHAPTER FIVE

"Wait up!" Jase shouted after the two women. He nudged Sherlock on the settee. "Come on, lazy."

Sherlock opened one eye. Realizing they were going for a walk, he flopped off the settee and followed Jase out.

On the way, they passed a caravan with a Jamaican flag flying overhead. Dancehall music boomed through the open windows. Inside, Jase glimpsed a large group of people, all chatting and laughing.

A boy emerged, the music getting even louder as he opened the door.

"Be back before dinner!" a woman's voice called out after him. "You're cooking!"

"I know!" he shouted back, jumping down the steps in one go.

He was one of the kids Jase had seen playing basketball on the way in. He was about Jase's age, ten, maybe eleven. His hair was shaved at the sides in sharp, zig-zagged lines, with a bundle of Afro curls on top. He was wearing a white T-shirt, so bright Jase had to squint to look at him, over a pair of knee-length shorts and the second coolest pair of creps Jase had ever seen. (In his opinion, he was wearing the number one coolest.) They were white with neon-coloured stripes on the soles. And they didn't have a single crease in them. Which reminded Jase: he needed to get some crease guards for his.

The boy turned to them, clocked Jase's trainers, and smiled.

"Those Jordans are wavy," he said, pointing at Jase's shoes.

Jase beamed. He'd never had anyone compliment any of his clothes before. "Thanks. Yours are fresh too."

"Thanks. These are my second faves. I'd love an

40

OG style like yours, but Mum says six pairs of trainers is enough!"

"Six!" Jase said.

"I do chores for the whole family to pay for them. And I have a BIG family." He gestured over his shoulder with a thumb to the caravan behind him. "My mum, dad and four sisters are in there. That one's my auntie's," he said, pointing to the caravan next to his. "That belongs to my other auntie. And my two uncles have ones over there." He pointed out three more caravans. Five caravans in total.

"That's a big family!"

"They're all here. And they're ALL loud. I'm escaping to the Coast if you want to come?"

Jase turned to look at Nicki.

"Go on! Have fun!" She shooed him away.

"Sure?" he said, looking at his nana.

"Perfect," his nana said. "It means we can go to the pub. They don't let littluns in there."

He gave her a quick hug and turned back to his new friend. "Should I grab my swimming trunks?"

The boy looked momentarily confused, and then laughed. But not in a way that made Jase feel silly. It was a nice, warm laugh. "Sorry. I meant the Gold Coast – the arcade."

"Cool!" *Even better,* Jase thought. He wasn't a very good swimmer. "I'm Jase, by the way."

"Tyrone," Tyrone said, laying his hand on his chest. Sherlock barked.

"And this is Sherlock."

Tyrone bent down in front of the dog and patted him on the head. "Nice to meet you, Sherlock."

Sherlock gave Tyrone's hand a quick lick, which meant he approved of him.

The two boys turned to leave when the door to Tyrone's caravan opened again. A little girl came out. Jase recognized her as the girl who had waved at him on the way in. She couldn't have been older than five.

"Ty, Ty!" she said. "Will you play pirates with me?" She waved a plastic sword in his direction.

"When I come back, Femi, I promise."

"You promise?" She couldn't pronounce her Rs

42

properly, so promise came out like *pwomise*. Jase thought it was super cute.

"You have my word, or you can cut me down like the scallywag I am," Tyrone said, in a drawling pirate accent.

She giggled. "Arrrgh!" she said.

"Arrrgh!" Tyrone said, waving back at her as he and Jase set off. Sherlock padded on ahead, sniffing the path.

Jase immediately liked Tyrone. He hadn't been embarrassed playing with his little sister in front of a new boy, the way Jase's own brothers would have been.

"Where are you from?" Tyrone asked.

"Nottingham."

"No way! Derby." He pointed to himself.

Jase knew it but had never been. He jabbed a thumb at his chest. "Beeston."

"And is this your first time at Castle Rock?" Tyrone asked.

"Yup."

"You're going to love it! We come here every summer. The whole family. Dad works in construction so he's away a lot on big projects. He says he loves spending quality time with everyone. But all he does is sleep."

Jase laughed. "I'm here with my auntie and nana. My mum's back at home. I bet she's sleeping loads too."

"They seem cool. Your aunt and nana."

"My nana has Alzheimer's," Jase blurted out. He didn't know where that had come from.

Tyrone stopped walking and looked at Jase, giving him his full attention. "What's Alzheimer's?"

Jase had never spoken to anyone outside his family about this before. Not even his best friends knew what had been going on. He tried his best to explain. "It's a type of dementia that makes it hard to remember things and make decisions. So, like, my nana, she struggles to remember things some days. Or can't work out how to do simple stuff like put her coat on. So, I try to help her."

Tyrone laid a hand on Jase's shoulder. "Oh, man, that sounds really tough."

Jase had never stopped to think about how all of it

had affected him. He'd been more worried about Nana Rose and his mum. But it hadn't been easy, and he got sad about it sometimes.

"A bit, I guess. My biggest worry is that she'll forget who I am. Every day we're losing a little bit more of her. My mum calls it the 'long goodbye'."

"I can't imagine," Tyrone said.

Jase scratched the back of his head, trying to distract himself from the wave of sadness that was building up in his belly. "It's OK. For now, we're making the most of every day! And she's great. She used to be a police detective and tells the best stories. Like, she once found this severed finger in a bin!"

"Ewww!" Tyrone said as they started walking again.

"Exactly! She knew something was up. Why hadn't the person the finger belonged to gone to a hospital? Why hadn't anyone reported it? The only thing she had to go on was that the finger had a gold sovereign ring on it. So she went to every jeweller's in Nottingham, showing them pictures of this ring, until she tracked down who it belonged to."

"And whose was it?" Tyrone said, sounding gripped.

"It belonged to a butcher called Trevor," Jase said, speaking so quickly now his words tumbled over each other. "She went to speak to him about his hand and when she turned up, he panicked and took a swing at her with his butcher's knife! She wrestled him to the floor and got the knife off him. Turns out he was selling dodgy meat and he thought she'd found him out! She cuffed him and marched him down to the station." Jase sucked in air. He'd been talking so much he'd run out of breath.

He'd only ever listened to his nana's stories before. But it was almost as much fun telling them.

"She sounds awesome!" Tyrone said. And he meant it. "You should write those stories down!"

Jase had never thought about this. About what would happen to Nana's stories when she was gone.

"That is a brilliant idea!"

"Thanks, I am full of them!" Tyrone grinned. "And here we are."

They had stopped in front of a single-storey white

building with flashing neon signs in the windows. From inside, Jase heard the noises of bells ringing and coins dropping.

"As far as we're concerned," Tyrone said, "this is the best arcade in Skeggy."

"We?" Jase asked.

"The Castle Rock Caravan Crew," Tyrone said.

CHAPTER SIX

"Welcome to the Coast," Tyrone said, as proud as if he'd built the arcade himself.

It took Jase's eyes a little while to adjust to the lighting inside. The room was about the size of his classroom at school. It was filled with all kinds of old video game machines, all flashing and pumping out looping snippets of music. There was a football table and a small pool table to the side of the room, and in the middle was a large coin pusher machine, the kind where you put a 2p in and hope it pushes a load of other 2ps out.

The walls were painted with a graffiti mural of gaming characters on a beach. Mario was jumping over

space invader aliens on a surfboard, while Sonic the Hedgehog was making a sandcastle out of Minecraft bricks. Painted with their backs to the viewer were four kids. Two girls and two boys. One of them had a haircut that looked very similar to Tyrone's.

"Is that you?" Jase asked, pointing at the figure.

"Yeah, we painted that last summer," Tyrone said, smiling. "Someone broke in and scrawled rubbish graffiti all over the place and broke some of the machines. But we put it all right."

"Who would do that?"

"It's a mystery we have yet to solve! But we reckon it was one of the local kids. They get annoyed at us holidaymakers."

Jase looked back at the mural. "It's great."

"Kinga did most of it. The rest of us helped."

"Kinga?"

"Come on, meet the crew."

Tyrone led the way over to two girls, who looked about Jase's age. One was playing a driving game, throwing her whole body into each turn. The other was engrossed in watching something on her phone.

Tyrone greeted the second girl with a complicated handshake, which she completed without even looking up from her phone. It started with a hand slap and fist bump and ended with clicking fingers and pointing at each other. It was one of the coolest things Jase had ever seen.

"Kinga, meet Jase," Tyrone said.

The girl looked up from her phone at last and gave

him a bright smile. "Hey, Jase."

She had light brown hair pulled back into a tight ponytail that fell down to the middle of her back. She was wearing a pink bomber jacket, which was covered in badges, over a purple dress. Cat-eye sunglasses were propped on her head. And her wrists jingled with bracelets and bands of all different colours.

"Yes!" the other girl shouted. "Highest score, suckers."

Jase watched as the girl inputted three letters to mark her place on the top of the leader board: HRI.

She jumped out of the driver's seat. She too greeted Tyrone with *the* handshake.

"And this is Harri," Tyrone said.

Harri was wearing a baggy green boiler suit with the sleeves tied around her waist. Under it, she had a blue T-shirt with "Take Up Space" written over a picture of a rocket shooting past the stars. She had Converse trainers that might once have been white but were now covered in different coloured paint speckles. Her blonde hair was gathered up in messy space buns. One was dyed purple, the other was dyed bright pink.

"How long were you playing?" Tyrone asked.

"A whole hour," Kinga said, sounding unimpressed.

"No way! It felt more like ten minutes!" Harri said, looking at her watch. "Guess that's hyperfocusing for you."

Jase looked confused.

"Harri has ADHD," Tyrone explained. "Mostly, it means she has the attention span of a distracted squirrel."

Harri opened her mouth to protest and then thought better of it. "Yeah, OK, that's fair."

"But when she's hyperfocused on something she likes, she loses track of time."

"Comes in handy, though, for SMASHING your brother's top score."

She shouted this in the direction of the only other person in the arcade – an older boy who was playing pinball. He was dressed head-to-toe in black, with brown hair that fell over his face. He didn't even look over at them.

The pinball machine made a sad *wha wah* game-over

sound. He slammed his hand against the side of it in frustration.

"Don't mind him, that's just my BORING big brother, Oliver. He used to be one of the crew. And then he started hanging out with the BORING townie kids. And even they think he's too BORING."

Jase looked over to the mural. He recognized Tyrone, Harri and Kinga in the painting. The fourth figure must have been Oliver, though in the painting he was wearing a bright orange baseball cap with the peak turned backwards, red shorts and a purple T-shirt. Now he was wearing all black. Jase wondered what had happened to all the colour.

"Shut up, *Harriet*!" Oliver called back. He kicked the pinball machine and slouched his way out of the arcade.

"It's HARRI!" Harri yelled after him, stamping her foot.

"Who's this?" Kinga said, looking down at Sherlock. He'd been sitting quietly, watching everything.

Jase introduced Sherlock to the girls and told them he was a beagle. They promptly knelt down and started cooing over how cute he was. He rolled over and allowed them to give him belly rubs.

"I want a dog," Harri said. "I've only got two guinea pigs. Armstrong and Aldrin. You know, after the first men on the moon."

"Harri is going to work for the UK Space Agency and build the first rocket that goes to Mars, isn't that right?" Tyrone said.

"Venus!" she said. "They're already working on the Mars rocket."

"Venus, right!" Tyrone said. "And Kinga here is going to work for the UN and save the world from fast fashion."

Kinga was back looking at her phone. With her spare hand she was making flowing gestures, as if learning the moves to a dance.

"If she can ever stop watching TikTok."

Kinga stuck her tongue out at Tyrone.

"How about you, Jase? You have a life plan?" Harri asked.

Jase felt himself blush as all eyes turned on him.

"Well, I … I want to be a police detective."

Jase was used to people scrunching up their noses when he said this. The police weren't that popular back on his estate.

"And bring criminals to justice!" Kinga said. "Cool."

Jase smiled. He'd tried to explain to his friends at school why he wanted to join the police, and they didn't understand. But this girl he'd just met, she'd instantly got it.

"You all have a plan!" Tyrone said, throwing his hands up. "My older sisters are the same. One is going to be a vet. The other is training to be a make-up artist. Me, I have absolutely no idea what I'm going to do."

"You're going to play basketball for the Leicester Riders," Kinga said. "And when you retire, you're going to open a restaurant. He's the best cook!" She directed this last bit at Jase.

"I'm glad someone has my life figured out!"

"I thought you were going to be a pirate," Jase said with a grin.

Tyrone laughed. "Yeah, man, I might just! Arrrgh!"

Sherlock was wandering around the room having a good sniff and snaffling up any crumbs people had dropped on the floor.

"Hey," Harri said, "I've just realized. There are four of us."

"Oooh, yes!" Kinga said.

Jase didn't know what was going on.

"Foosball!" the three of them said at the same time.

They ran over to a table in the corner. Jase and Sherlock followed them.

Rows of little footballers hung over the green pitch with poles through their sides. One team was dressed in red, the other in blue. The table looked a bit dusty.

Harri put her hand on one of the handles and gave the row of men a *spin*. "Oliver used to play with us, before he became so boring!" she said.

"You can be on my team," Kinga said, standing on the red side. Jase was pleased. His team were Nottingham Forest and they wore red.

Jase had only played table football once before. But he got the hang of it pretty quickly. You had to twist the pole to make your men kick the ball into the opposition's goal, while stopping the ball from going into your goal. Though the group had lots of rules he didn't know. Like spinning was banned, so you couldn't just make your men go round and round in circles. And if the ball got stuck so that no one could touch it, it was taken out of play, but instead of being thrown back in through the usual slide, one of the players threw it into the middle with their eyes closed. Lobs, when the ball goes over the goal bar and scores, were worth two points. And the goalie was then allowed to spin upside down to try and stop it.

It was fast and frantic, and Jase wasn't that good. But it didn't matter because Kinga was amazing. She could pass the ball back and forth between her players and make it bounce on their feet. The others were good too, though Harri kept trying to cheat by doing things like blowing on the ball, which she kept saying was recreating harsh weather conditions.

Sherlock played too. When the ball bounced off the table, he would chase it down and bring it back to the group. The slobber, they decided, made the game even better.

After playing for ages, Jase was hot and sweaty, but he had scored two goals and stopped the other side from scoring three. Kinga said this made him the best goalie ever.

It was down to the last ball. The score was five all. Harri dropped the ball into play. It bounced twice. There was a frenzy of flying foosball feet. The ball bounced off the side and went flying towards Jase's goal. Everything seemed to slow down. Jase slammed his pole forward. The ball stopped dead by his goalie's feet. With a flick of his wrist, he sent the ball soaring, high over the heads of the other little football payers.

With a satisfying *THUNK* it landed in the opposite goal.

His team had won!

Kinga gave him a double high five. Tyrone shook his hand. Harri wasn't such a good loser, but after some encouragement from the others, she admitted he was a very skilled player.

"Be on my team next time!" Harri whispered when Tyrone wasn't looking.

Harri cheered herself up after losing by having one last go on the racing game. She managed to beat her last score, so her initials appeared twice on the leader board, pushing her brother even further down.

"It's already six!" Tyrone said, looking at his watch.

How was that possible? It had only felt like an hour since he had arrived. But it had been nearly four! He'd been having so much fun he hadn't looked at his watch once.

"I was wondering what that noise was," Harri said, her hand pressed against her stomach. "It was my belly rumbling!"

Now that Jase thought about it, his was grumbling as well.

"Come on then, Sherlock. Let's get you fed."

CHAPTER SEVEN

Walking back to their caravans, Tyrone, Harri and Kinga gave a running commentary on everything they passed.

"That's Mr Collins, the site manager," Tyrone said, pointing at a man who was wandering in circles, his eyes fixed on the ground.

"You lost something, Mr Collins?" Kinga shouted out.

The man looked up, startled. He had a plump face, large eyes, and a short white beard. He was wearing shorts, sandals over socks and a vest. Something about him made Jase think of Santa Claus on his summer holiday.

"No," Mr Collins said quickly. "Nothing." He waddled off, glancing back at them over his shoulder every few steps.

"Well, that was weird," Tyrone said. "He's usually really friendly."

"Maybe he's forgotten where he parked his sleigh," Jase said. It was the kind of joke his aunt would have made. The split second after he said it, he wished he could suck it back into his mouth. But they all laughed.

"Sleigh!" Tyrone said, chuckling. "He does look like Santa!"

"You're funny!" Kinga said.

Jase grinned to himself. He'd never been called funny before.

"That's the launderette," Harri said, pointing across the road to a small white building. "But make sure you only use the machine on the far left, the others all eat your pants."

"And that's the site shop," Kinga said, as they passed a glass-fronted convenience store. "You can get everything in there."

"Everything?" Jase asked.

"Everything!" the other three answered.

As they walked past, the big glass doors slid open to release the smell of fresh bread and plastic beachballs.

Jase would have to explore tomorrow.

An old woman emerged from the shop, carrying a net bag filled with sausages and tins of baked beans. It was the same woman Jase had seen crossing the road earlier.

"All right, dustbin lids," the old woman said. She had a strong cockney accent and spoke out of the side of her mouth.

"Hi, Beryl," Kinga said.

The others waved.

"Hope you're not getting up to no mischief," she said.

"Us? Never!" Tyrone replied.

The old woman gave a snort of disbelief and shuffled off.

"Dustbin lids?" Jase asked.

"Dustbin lids, kids," Kinga translated. "It's cockney

rhyming slang. Though we think she just puts it on for effect."

"We heard her talking on the phone once, and she talked posh as anything," Harri said.

Jase watched the hunched figure make her way down the winding path. "Mysterious."

"This place is filled with mysteries," Kinga said. "That's one of the best things about it."

Speaking of mysteries. "Who lives there?" Jase asked, pointing at a camper van standing on its own, away from the others. No flag flew outside and it was surrounded by tall weeds. The only sign of life was a small orange light glowing in one of the windows.

"Oh, we don't go near that," Kinga whispered.

"It's haunted," Tyrone said.

"There is absolutely no scientific evidence for ghosts," Harri said loudly, as if daring any ghost that might be around to prove her wrong.

"Cursed then," Kinga said.

"No such thing as curses."

"Oh yeah? Then why wouldn't you knock when we

dared you last year?" Kinga asked.

"Because…" Harri said, struggling to think of an excuse. "Because it's rude to just go banging on people's doors and running away!"

"Pfff!" Kinga said, not believing a word of it. "You were as scared of the bogeyman as the rest of us."

"And there is no such thing as bogeymen either!" Harri said.

"It's creepy," Jase said.

The air around the camper van seemed darker somehow. As if shrouded in its own cloud.

"On that, we can agree," Harri said.

And they hurried on quickly.

"Mum's looking for you, Harriet." A boy was leaning out of a caravan window: the boy from the arcade. Harri's older brother Oliver. His message delivered, he slammed the window shut.

"It's *Harri*," Harri said through gritted teeth.

"He only does it to annoy you," Kinga said.

"It's working."

The caravan had a black-and-white checked flag flying over it and a bright yellow car parked outside. The car had the number 52 painted on the side. Half the engine appeared to be on the ground. Sherlock sniffed at the engine parts, but quickly decided that none of it could be eaten.

There was a strange, muffled sound coming from underneath the car.

"What?" Harri said.

A man slid out from between the car's wheels. "I said hand me the socket wrench, could ya?"

Harri bent over a red toolbox and picked out a tool with a round head, which she handed to the man.

"This is my dad," she said.

He had a curly beard and even curlier hair. Like Harri, he wore overalls, though his were drenched in oil. His arms were covered in tattoos, including one which read "Oliver" and another which clearly used to read "Harriet", but a line had been drawn through the last two letters, so now it read "Harri".

He waved the wrench in their general direction, then slid back under the car. Jase reckoned he must be lying on a skateboard or something.

"There you are! I told Oliver that I was looking for you."

They turned to see a woman emerging from a very small caravan opposite the one with the car.

The woman had long blonde hair pulled up into a high bun. She was wearing bright pink sliders which matched her bright pink nails, a pair of denim shorts and a white vest top. Her skin was the brown of someone who spent a lot of time in the sun, and her teeth the white of someone who took very good care of them.

"And this is my mum," Harri said.

The woman approached and instantly adjusted Harri's hair, tucking strands that had come loose back into place.

"Hey, Tyrone and Kinga," she said with a *dazzling* smile. "Excited for the summer?"

"Yes, Mrs Coston."

"How many times, kids? Call me Arlette. Besides, it's Ms now. And who is your new friend?" She spoke almost as quickly as Harri did.

"This is Jase. It's his first time at Castle Rock."

"Welcome to the family, Jase," Arlette said. "Dinner's almost ready. Guy has made steamed fish and salad."

A young man opened the door of the caravan and stepped out on to the veranda. He had to duck under the doorway to get through. Jase was surprised he didn't have to turn sideways as well. He was one of the biggest men he had ever seen.

"Salmon!" he said, with a smile almost as bright as Harri's mum's. "Rich in omega-3. Good for your muscles." As if to prove his point, the man flexed an arm. He could have cracked walnuts with those biceps.

"Oh, I told Dad I'd eat with him tonight. Isn't that right, Dad?" Harri said.

"Huh?" The reply came from under the car. Harri's dad slid out again. His face seemed to have even more oil on it this time.

"I said I'd *promised* to eat with *you* tonight," Harri said, stressing every word.

"You did…?" At last, Harri's dad seemed to get the message being beamed at him from Harri's eyes like lasers. "Oh, yes. You did! I really wanted Harri to eat with me tonight, if that's OK, Arlette?" He stood up and wrapped his hand around Harri's shoulder, leaving an oily mark. Harri didn't seem to mind.

"Oh, of course," her mum said with a brittle smile. "Of course. But no takeaway, OK?" She wagged a finger at Harri and her dad. "And I get you for breakfast."

"As long as it's not fish," Harri muttered under her breath.

Arlette gave her daughter's hair one last adjustment, then walked back up the steps to the caravan. The giant man waved them goodnight, then he ducked back inside and closed the door.

"We know," Tyrone said in a whisper. "How does he fit in such a small caravan?"

That was *exactly* what Jase had been thinking.

"Thanks, Dad," Harri said. "You saved me from steamed salmon. Yuck!"

"Guy's a good … um, guy, you know," Harri's dad said, giving her a playful pop on the jaw.

"He's so boring! All he does is lift weights and eat protein. He tried to get me to do ten burpees when we arrived yesterday! Burpees, Dad! Me?!"

"We thought she was going to have a heart attack," Kinga said.

She pulled something up on her phone and showed it to Jase. It was a video of Harri lying on the floor, her arms and legs splayed out like a jellyfish.

"I told you to delete that!" Harri said, swiping at Kinga's phone. But Kinga was too quick and snatched it away. "I will. I just need to watch it a couple more … thousand times."

Harri's dad laughed. "Give Guy a chance, Harri. He makes your mum very happy."

"And who is going to make you happy, Dad?" Harri said, looking down at her feet as she kicked at a stone on the floor.

"Doris," he said.

"Who?" Harri said excitedly.

Her dad moved back to the car and patted the bright yellow paintwork. "Doris!"

Harri sighed heavily and shook her head. "Come on," she said. "I'll order the takeaway. See you all tomorrow."

Harri gave Kinga and Tyrone The Handshake (Jase thought it deserved capital letters) and slouched inside the caravan.

"Harri's parents got divorced when she was little," Kinga said, as they continued their walk back to their sites. "They come down to Castle Rock as a family each year and always get on brilliantly."

"But this year," Tyrone said, "her mum brought her new boyfriend."

"Her hot, *younger* boyfriend," Kinga added.

"And now Harri's worried that her dad will be lonely."

"That must be hard," Jase said.

His parents had divorced when he was little too. He didn't see his dad that much as he'd re-married and moved to Manchester. But he liked his stepmum and stepsister just fine.

Tyrone shrugged. "Her mum and dad will work it out. They always do."

CHAPTER EIGHT

The remaining three (four counting Sherlock) moved on a little further and approached another caravan. This one looked more like a Swiss chalet than a caravan. The walls were covered in light wood panelling and there were large glass windows on two sides. It even had a sloping roof.

"Kinga has the fanciest caravan," Tyrone said.

A red-and-white flag flew overhead.

"It's the Polish flag," Kinga said, seeing Jase gazing up at it. "You wanna see inside?"

"Sure!" Jase said. He was curious to see if it was as fancy inside as it was outside.

They walked up the wooden steps to the large glass

doors. Kinga stopped, her hand on the handle, and turned back to them. "Just don't eat anything my dad offers you."

"Why not?" Jase asked.

"You'll see," Kinga said.

They had been right about this place being full of mystery.

Inside, the caravan looked like something out of a magazine. Crisp white settee with bright scatter cushions. Grey plush rugs lay over wooden flooring. A bright white kitchen took up half of the open-plan room. Jase knew his mum would kill for a kitchen like that at home.

"Stay," Jase said to Sherlock. He wasn't sure if these people would want his stinky dog on their clean rugs.

Sherlock barked, then curled up on the welcome mat and kept watch.

A woman was sitting with her legs tucked under her on the settee. She had dark hair cut into a neat bob and was dressed in grey co-ord leggings and jumper and fluffy slippers. She was wearing two pairs of glasses — one perched on the end of her nose, the other on top of her head. She was busy chewing a pencil and staring at a crossword puzzle.

With a satisfied "ha!" she scribbled a word in the crossword box and threw the paper down on the glass coffee table.

"Hello!" she said, swapping one pair of glasses for the other. "Did you have a good day, sweetheart?"

"Great, thanks, Mum."

"Hello again, Mrs Pearce," Tyrone said.

"Hey, Tyrone," the woman replied. "Did you have a good year?"

"Not bad, Mrs P. Not bad."

"And I see someone else here has passed the vibe check."

"Please don't use slang, Mum. You never get it right," Kinga said. "Jase, meet my mum; Mum, meet Jase."

"Pleased to meet you, Jase."

"And Dad…"

A man was standing in the kitchen. He spun around like a magician ready to reveal a trick. He had dark hair, cut in a neat, sharp style, and was wearing a grey tracksuit and fluffy slippers that matched his wife's. He was carrying a plate of what looked like chocolate balls on one outstretched hand.

"Well, hello there," he said. "Chocolate truffle anyone?" He pushed the plate under Kinga's nose.

Kinga picked one up. She raised it to her mouth and then stopped. "Let me guess," she said. "Brussels sprouts covered in chocolate?"

She threw the ball back on the plate.

"Damn it! You always catch me out!" Kinga's dad said.

He put the plate down and walked over to a plant pot. He pulled a phone out from the leaves. He must have hidden it there, hoping to catch Kinga's reaction on video.

"My dad's trying to become TikTok famous," Kinga explained, rolling her eyes to the ceiling.

"And how's that working out, Mr P?" Tyrone asked.

"Well, she hasn't fallen for one of my pranks yet!"

"And you've fallen for every one of hers!" Kinga's mum said.

Kinga's dad shook his fist playfully at the sky, as if cursing the gods of TikTok. He then grabbed Kinga around the waist and bundled her on to the settee next to his wife. Snuggled between her parents, Jase noticed that Kinga didn't really look like either her mum or dad. They had tanned skin and dark eyes, whereas she was pale and had bright blue eyes. All three of them had the same big smiles, though.

"Are you staying for dinner, boys?" Kinga's dad asked.

"And risk more Brussels sprouts?" Kinga said. "Run!"

They all laughed.

"No thanks, Mr P," Tyrone said. "I have to get back and cook."

He stretched his hand out to Kinga and they pulled off The Handshake again. Jase watched carefully, trying to see how it was done, but they were too fast and smooth, and it was over in a flash.

"I'd better head home too," Jase said.

"See you tomorrow," Kinga said.

Sherlock bounced up when they joined him outside.

"So, you guys have known each other for ages then?" Jase said, as he and Tyrone walked back to their own caravans.

"Harri and I have been coming here for, like, six years. This is Kinga's third year. The four of us make up the Castle Rock Caravan Crew."

"Oh, cool."

They were a tight gang. And for the first time since meeting them all, Jase felt like a bit of an outsider.

"It's a bit cheesy, but you'll get used to it."

"I ... what?"

"Well, you're the newest member."

"I am?"

"Of course!" Tyrone said. "Mrs P was right. You passed the vibe check."

Jase and Tyrone laughed.

"And what does being a member of the Castle Rock Caravan Crew involve?"

"You know, we hang out together, solve mysteries,

that kind of thing."

"Mysteries?"

"When we can find them. Oh, and of course there's this."

He reached out his hand. Jase felt a ripple of excitement in his stomach. Was he really going to learn The Handshake?

It took Jase two goes to get it right.

"There. Now you're a fully-fledged member of the Castle Rock Crew."

Jase beamed. Even though the air was cooler now, he felt like his cheeks were glowing.

Tyrone leaned down to Sherlock and reached out a hand. Sherlock gave him his paw and Tyrone shook it. "And so is Sherlock!"

"No fair!" It was Femi, her face squeezed between the posts of Tyrone's caravan. "I wanna join."

"And you will, when you're older."

"But I wanna join now!" She threw her head back and wailed.

Tyrone rushed over and tried to hush Femi.

"Stop upsetting your sister," a voice shouted from inside.

"Stay out of this, Amelia!" Tyrone shouted back. "That's my big sister," he said to Jase. And then mimed a big nose.

"I heard that," the voice called back.

Tyrone ignored his big sister and turned back to his little one. "How about I promise you can join the crew next year?"

"And..." Femi said, opening a negotiation.

"And ... I promise to win you a cuddly toy from Fantasy Island tomorrow?"

Femi considered this. "A big one?"

"The biggest."

Femi pursed her lips and then nodded. "OK."

She took Tyrone's hand and started to tug her brother back inside. "So, Fantasy Island tomorrow morning?" Tyrone said over his shoulder as he was being dragged away.

"Sure," Jase said. He couldn't wait to go on his first roller coaster.

He practically skipped back to his caravan, Sherlock by his side.

"Hey!" Nicki said as they returned. "You had fun?"

"The most fun."

"What did I tell you?" his nana said. "Best place on the planet."

Jase hadn't been to that many places on the planet. Yet. But of the ones he had been to, Castle Rock was certainly in his top five.

"And to make it even better," Nicki said, "we're going out for pizza!"

When they got back later, Jase was tired and happy and looking forward to sleeping without his brother snoring in the same room. He was pretty sure this was the best birthday he'd ever had.

He yawned and looked around for his birthday coin. He wanted to show it to Tyrone in the morning.

"Where's my present?" he asked his nana.

"Your what, love?" she said. She was applying her night cream and her face looked like a clown's, although Jase never told her that.

"The coin that you gave me. It was right there." He pointed at the empty spot on the sideboard.

"Don't ask me. I have dementia, you know." She laughed her husky laugh.

Jase kissed her on her cheek, wiped the night cream off his nose, and went to bed. The mystery of the vanishing coin could wait until tomorrow.

CHAPTER NINE

He and Tyrone were due to meet at 10 a.m., and it was already quarter past.

Maybe he's forgotten, Jase thought. *Maybe something has happened to him? Maybe he's been abducted by aliens!*

Jase looked up when he heard his name being called. It was Tyrone, waving him over to his caravan.

"Yo!" Tyrone said. There was no sign of any alien abduction that Jase could see. Tyrone was wearing a different pair of trainers from yesterday: all black apart from a red tick on the side. "Come in, they're nearly done."

What are nearly done? Jase wondered. As he walked into the caravan, he was hit by a delicious smell.

Ginger and nutmeg and coconut.

The caravan was around the same size as Nana Rose's, but whereas hers was stuck in the 80s, this place was the height of fashion. Abstract art was hung on the walls and geometric rugs and cushions had been placed perfectly around the living room. And there were so many plants it reminded Jase of when he'd gone on a school trip to the Birmingham botanical gardens.

Tyrone pulled on a pair of red oven gloves and opened the oven. The amazing smell became even stronger. Tyrone pulled out a tray of light-golden cake. "It's Jamaican Toto cake," he explained. "One of my specialities."

He tipped the cake out on to a rack and cut it into slices. He handed one to Jase.

Jase blew on it and took a bite. It was one of the best things he had ever tasted. Sweet and chewy and yum.

"It's AMAZING," Jase said, before he'd even finished eating.

"Thanks. It's my great-aunt Chandice's recipe. I'm the only one in the family she trusted with it."

"Which is totally unfair!"

A tall girl with neat braids falling loose around her shoulders emerged from the back of the caravan. She was older than Tyrone, maybe sixteen or seventeen, but was unmistakably his sister. They had the same smile and intelligent deep brown eyes. Though hers were accented by perfect golden eyeshadow.

His sister tried to nick one of the slices. Tyrone slapped her hand away with a spatula. "They're for my friends."

"Aren't I your friend?" she said, pouting.

"This is Amelia, my older sister," Tyrone said. "She's supposed to be the smart one in the family."

"What's that?" She pointed out the window as if she'd seen something exciting. Both Jase and Tyrone looked to see.

There was nothing there. When they looked back, Amelia was eating one of Tyrone's cakes. "Smarter than you, little bro," she said, grabbing a magazine and wandering off again.

Tyrone started putting the cake slices in a Tupperware box.

"Doth my nose betray me, or is that Toto cake I can smell?" The back doors slid open and a broad man walked in.

He had long locs pulled back from his shoulders with a bright blue scarf.

"Don't know what you mean, Dad. I can't smell anything!" Tyrone said, quickly putting all the remaining slices into the box and putting the lid on.

"Just one, please!" Tyrone's dad put his hands together and pleaded. He had a warm Liverpudlian accent and Jase immediately liked him. He had the same big smile as his son.

"OK, just one." He peeled open the lid and allowed his dad to take one out. "But don't tell Mum."

"Don't tell your mother what?" A tall, slim woman appeared. Her hair was wrapped up in a green-and-yellow scarf which was tied in a knot at the top of her head. Her movements were slow and graceful.

Tyrone rolled his eyes and handed over the box. "Toto cake," he said. It seemed there was no point trying to hide anything from his mum.

She took a slice and bit down into it, her eyes closed. "Almost as good as your auntie used to make." She had the hint of a Jamaican accent.

"Almost?" Tyrone said, offended.

"Yes. Needs more ginger."

Tyrone made a *harumph* noise as he closed the box and tucked it under his arm. "If you're all done stealing my cake, I'm off to Fantasy Island. Oh, and this is Jase. Jase, these are my cake-thieving parents!"

Tyrone's dad reached his hands out as if he was going to steal the cake box. Tyrone ducked out of the way and ran for the door. Jase followed.

"Have a good time!" Tyrone's mum called after them.

"Don't be sick!" his dad shouted. "Would be a waste of good Toto cake!"

Jase laughed. Tyrone's dad reminded him of his auntie Nicki. He reckoned the two of them would get on.

Tyrone pulled an electric scooter from around the back of the caravan, and pushed it, the cake box balanced on the handlebars.

They were meeting the others outside the Coast. Kinga was just pulling up as they arrived.

"*Ooooh*, Toto cake!"

She climbed off a pink bike with a wicker basket. Tyrone gave her a slice and she ate it, slowly picking little crumbs off it to make it last as long as possible. Jase was already regretting eating his so quickly. He wondered how many slices Tyrone had left.

Kinga had her hair down today and she was wearing a red leavers' hoodie. Backwards.

"Um…" Jase said, pointing at it.

"Oh, yes," Kinga said, taking her arms out of the sleeves and turning it back around the right way. "I pulled the hoodie trick on my dad this morning. You know the one: you stand in front of a fridge with your hoodie on backwards and the hood up, and when they think they're sneaking up on you … bam! You grab 'em. I scared the life out of him!"

She showed the boys the video she'd captured. She wasn't wrong. Her dad had jumped straight in the air and squealed like a kitten when she pounced.

"That's going on TikTok later."

"Where's Harri?" Tyrone asked.

They looked around and couldn't see any sign of her coming down the path.

"She probably got caught up in something. Or she's still in bed. Let's swing by her caravan and see if we can surprise her!"

Before they even got to her caravan, they heard shouting from inside.

"Where is it?" That was Harri.

"I don't know what you're talking about!" That was her brother, Oliver.

"Stop shouting, both of you. You'll wake everyone up!" Harri's dad shouted louder than either of his children.

Jase and the others approached. The door to the caravan was open. They peered inside.

Every surface of the caravan was filled with all sorts of machinery and engine parts. There were circuit boards stacked on the dining table. Cogs and pistons on the sideboards. The kitchen was just a kettle, a single gas hob and a small sink. The sink was black with oil and the whole place smelled of petrol. It looked more like a mechanic's garage than a holiday home.

Harri was standing in the middle of the room, her face bright red and her fists on her hips, staring at her brother. He was in the middle of eating a bowl of cornflakes and trying to watch the TV.

"I know you took my Switch!" she shouted at him.

"I told you," he said, leaning to the side so he could see past her, "I have no idea what you're talking about."

"Daaaaaddddd!"

"Harri, if he says he doesn't know, he doesn't know. You probably just lost it in your bedroom. It's a pigsty in there."

If Harri's room was even messier than the rest of the caravan, Jase wasn't surprised she might have lost something in there.

"It was in my bag yesterday morning. And now it's gone. And I saw HIM sniffing around it." She jabbed a finger in Oliver's direction.

"Get that out of my face." He swatted her finger away with the back of his spoon.

"I wish we had popcorn," Kinga said, clearly enjoying the drama.

"Maybe you left it in your mum's caravan," Harri's dad said. "You might have taken it with you when you had breakfast there."

Harri opened her mouth to protest and then seemed to reconsider.

"Guy did say he wanted to play on it."

"Well, there you go then. Go shout at him. I haven't had my coffee yet."

Harri spun around on her heels and stormed out the door and, not even saying good morning to the others, stomped over to her mum's caravan.

The others followed in her path like the trail of a meteor.

"Mum!" she shouted, throwing the door open.

There was no answer.

She strode through the caravan and straight out the back door. Jase and the others shared a quick glance. Tyrone and Kinga leaned their scooter and bike on the floor, and they followed.

Harri's mum's caravan couldn't have looked more different from her dad's. It was an explosion of colour. Everywhere were brightly coloured scatter cushions and glass animals. Pink glass pigs and rainbow glass unicorns, brown glass dogs and orange glass kittens. Jase was nervous to move too quickly in case he knocked one of them over.

On the patch of grass behind the caravan, they found Harri's mum. She was sunbathing, holding a book out in front of her. Jase twisted his head so he could read the cover. *Becoming* by Michelle Obama.

Guy was sitting on the end of her sun lounger, lifting a hand weight, while a small speaker on the floor played soft Jazz.

"Have you seen my Switch?" Harri asked Guy.

He put the weight down and thought. It looked like

hard work for him. "It's red and blue and about this big." He held his hands about a foot apart.

"I know what it looks like!" Harri said exasperatedly. "I can't find it. Did I leave it here this morning?"

Her mum propped herself up on her elbow. "No, sweetie, you didn't have it. Are you sure it's not in your room? I don't know how you find anything in that mess."

"It's not in my room," Harri said, though some of the certainty was leaving her voice.

"I'm sure it will turn up. Besides, aren't you heading to Fantasy Island today? Morning all." Harri's mum gave the group a small wave.

They returned it.

"The games at Fantasy Island are way better than Switch games," Guy said.

"That's not the point," Harri said. "I just don't like people touching my stuff. I have a system. And you mess with my system and my head gets all…" Harri mimed her head exploding.

"Of course, sweetie. Look, why don't you and

your friends go have fun at Fantasy Island and when you get back, I'll help you tidy your room, and we'll find it. OK?"

"OK," Harri said.

"Look, here." Her mum reached into her handbag and pulled out her purse. She took out a fiver and handed it to Harri. "Just don't tell your brother."

This made Harri's shoulders relax a little. She finally seemed to realize that the others were standing behind her.

"Toto cake?" Tyrone said, handing over the box.

This put a big smile on Harri's face. She grabbed the cake and ate it even quicker than Jase had done.

"Better?" Kinga asked.

"A bit."

"Fantasy Island will cheer you up," Tyrone said.

"Let me grab my skateboard."

As they started to walk back towards her caravan, Harri quickly pulled out a blue wallet, which was attached to her trousers by a chain. With a rip of Velcro, she opened it and neatly slipped the

five-pound note inside.

There was already a stash of other notes in there.

"Wow," Kinga said, spotting the cash.

Harri put the wallet away in her back pocket. "I've been saving up for Dad's birthday. I want to get him a remote-controlled car, but I don't have enough yet."

"Be careful walking around with it," Tyrone said.

"Safest place is with me," she said, patting her pocket.

She ducked inside her caravan and returned a moment later with a skateboard tucked under her arm. It had a picture of a spaceship painted on it.

It was only then that Jase realized something. He was the only one without a mode of transport. Tyrone had an electric scooter. Kinga had her bike. And Harri had a skateboard.

"Why don't we just walk today?" Tyrone said. He must have noticed too.

"Or you can borrow Oliver's old BMX?" Harri said. "He doesn't use it any more. Because all his COOL friends have electric scooters!" She shouted this last bit back through the door.

There was a mumbling from inside the caravan. Oliver telling Harri to shove off.

"Come on, it's over here."

"He won't mind?" Jase asked. He didn't want to cause even more trouble between Harri and her brother.

"Nah!" Harri yanked an old bike out from under the caravan. It was a bit rusty, and the tape around the handlebars was peeling off, but it rode fine.

"I hope you find your Switch," Jase said as they rode towards the site exit.

"Me too," Harri said. She was holding on to the back of Kinga's bike and being towed along.

"It's weird actually," Kinga said.

"What is?" Jase asked.

"My camera went missing yesterday. I thought Dad hid it as a joke, but he swears he didn't. I was going to have a proper look later, but what if it was stolen?"

"Hmmm…" said Jase, pulling on the brakes of his bike.

"Hmmm, what?" Harri said, letting go of Kinga's bike and skidding to a stop next to Jase.

"Oh, it's just that I had something go missing too. A coin my nana gave me for my birthday."

"OK, that *is* weird," Tyrone said, scooting around them in circles.

"It's probably just a coincidence."

"Or…" Tyrone looked over his shoulder.

They'd stopped near the creepy camper van. The one Tyrone said was haunted.

"You don't think…?" Kinga asked.

"Poltergeists have been known to move things," Jase said.

He'd watched a documentary about it once. This family had moved into a new house and their things kept being thrown around. They'd moved out a week later.

"What's a poltergeist?" Tyrone asked.

"A sort of ghost."

They stared at the camper van. Spiderwebs covered the windows, and Jase could swear he heard a low moaning from inside. He felt goosebumps break out on his skin, as if someone had just blown icy air on his arms.

"Come on," Harri said. "There's no such thing as poltergeists or bogeymen. My mum's probably right and I've just lost it in my messy room somewhere."

"What about my camera then? And Jase's coin?"

"I'm sure they'll all turn up." Harri pushed off with her skateboard and zoomed ahead.

Jase looked back at the creepy camper van. What if there *was* more to the missing things than just messy rooms and pranking dads? But it couldn't be a ghost, could it?

"Come on!" Tyrone shouted back, snapping Jase out of his thoughts.

He stood up on the pedals and quickly caught up with the others, trying to put the eerie camper van out of his mind.

CHAPTER TEN

As they got to the site exit, they heard more shouting. This time it was a group of people crowding around a short man with a round belly. They were all pointing fingers at him.

"Is that the site manager?" Jase asked.

"Yeah," Tyrone said.

"Why is everyone so cross at him?" Jase asked.

The others shrugged.

"Let's go find out, shall we?" Kinga said, pulling out her phone.

The crew pushed their way through the angry crowd until they got to the front.

"You said this site was secure!" a woman in a long flowery dress shouted.

"I've been coming here for twenty years. I may not be coming again!" a man in jean shorts and a pink vest top said.

Kinga started filming the scene, giving a running commentary as she did.

"Here we are at Castle Rock Caravan Park," she said, "where there seems to be a commotion. Residents are up in arms." She turned the phone in Mr Collins' direction. "Mr Collins, do you care to make a statement?"

"There's just been a bit of a misunderstanding," he said. "Please put that away."

He put his hand over her phone. Kinga lowered it but didn't stop filming.

Mr Collins looked very flustered. His cheeks were bright red and sweat dripped down his forehead.

"Misunderstanding?" the woman in the dress said. "I had twenty pounds taken from my caravan. How is *that* a misunderstanding?"

"And when did this happen?" Kinga asked, pointing the phone towards her.

"Last night!" she said. "I went out for dinner, and when I came back it was gone."

"And I had my watch stolen while I was in the shower!" a man said, pushing the first woman aside so he could be in the frame. He was wearing a grey tracksuit with a big gold chain.

"And my diamond earrings are gone," a woman shouted from the back.

"And my gnome!" the man in the jean shorts said, tapping Kinga on the shoulder. "Don't forget my gnome."

"I hope it's the one with its bum out," Harri said quietly. "I hate that thing."

Jase couldn't understand why anyone would want to steal a gnome, apart from as a joke? But everyone seemed to be taking it very seriously.

The group all started talking at once, shouting over each other, demanding that

Mr Collins take action.

Kinga was capturing it all as if she was a journalist at a war zone.

"Calm down, everyone," Mr Collins said. "Please, calm down."

"We need to get the police involved. I'm calling 999," the man in the tracksuit said.

There was a lot of nodding of heads and agreement from the people who'd had their items stolen.

"There's no need for that," Mr Collins said, sounding panicked. "I'm sure there's a simple explanation."

"There's only one explanation," the woman in the dress said. "There's a thief!"

There was a moment's silence as this sank in.

"Could you say that again, for the camera?" Kinga said.

The woman in the dress looked directly into Kinga's phone and said, "There is a thief at Castle Rock."

Kinga finally lowered her phone. She turned to the others and they all exchanged looks. Maybe there had been more to their missing things after all?

Auntie Nicki had said that Castle Rock was one of the safest places around. Where people left their doors open and everyone could relax. But now … if there was a thief?

"It's probably one of the local kids," someone at the back of the group said. "They're always here causing problems."

"Now, everyone, I will NOT have you throwing accusations around," Mr Collins said, his voice suddenly very serious. "If you would all make an orderly queue and ONE AT A TIME explain what has happened."

"Come on," Tyrone said. "Let's leave them to it."

"Do you think we should tell him about our missing things?" Kinga said.

"Later," Tyrone said. "It looks like it's going to be a while before he's finished listening to that lot."

They rode away, leaving Mr Collins taking people's statements.

"A thief. At Castle Rock!" Harri said. "I can't believe it."

"I guess you'll have to say sorry to Oliver," Tyrone said.

"Yeah ... let's not go overboard," Harri said. "He's still really annoying."

The sea breeze was cold on Jase's face as they rode along the coast. He'd been having the best time since arriving yesterday, but now something felt wrong. Like a stone in his shoe. There was a thief at work. And Jase wouldn't be properly settled until he knew they had been caught.

CHAPTER ELEVEN

It was a ten-minute ride alongside the beach to Fantasy Island.

Even for a Sunday, the town was packed. The four friends had to weave between holidaymakers heading for the beach with deckchairs tucked under their arms and towels thrown over their shoulders, and shopkeepers setting out their stalls, selling everything from rock sticks to wooden seagulls. They even passed a row of donkeys taking children for a ride up and down the beachfront. Jase didn't think the donkeys looked that happy about the arrangement.

With each step, the swooping, looping tracks of roller coasters got closer and closer. In the distance, they looked like a sculpture made by a kid out of coloured straws. Up close, they looked like some kind of giant, tentacled-robot creature attacking Skegness.

The sounds of screaming could be heard along with the cawing of seagulls. Jase could feel a squirm of nerves in his belly. Maybe he could give the roller coasters a miss and just watch the others? They'd need someone to hold their bags after all.

It was twenty-seven pounds to get a wristband that allowed you to go on all the rides. Nicki had given Jase the money, while his nana had slipped him an extra fiver so he could buy himself something to eat.

He hesitated before handing over the money at the booth. It was a lot. What if he went on one ride and hated it? What if he couldn't even make it on one ride?

The woman in the booth tapped her long, painted nails with impatience as he tried to decide. "You can always get the Little Explorer," she said, holding up a small wristband. The one for little kids.

"No," Jase said, determined, "I'll have the Discovery, please."

He handed over the crisp ten- and twenty-pound notes and slipped the bright green band around his wrist.

They walked through the turnstiles. Jase blinked in the sudden assault of sound and colour. Everywhere things flashed and shouted for his attention. Games to play. Rides to go on. People laughing and screaming and shouting.

"Let's go on Volcano first!" Harri shouted above the noise.

"What's Volcano?" Jase asked.

"You wait and wait and wait and then, bam, you're shot 55.7784 metres in the air at 50 miles per hour!"

Jase swallowed.

"Kinga's too short for Volcano," Tyrone said.

Jase noticed next to one of the rides was a wooden sign pointing out the minimum height restriction of 1.4 metres. Jase, Harri and Tyrone were all tall enough. But Kinga was the smallest in the group.

"I am not too short," Kinga said indignantly. "I've grown a whole centimetre this year. Besides, I'm wearing my wedge-heel trainers."

She stood next to the sign and elongated her neck as much as she could. She barely made it.

"Let's keep Volcano until the end," Tyrone said. "Just in case."

"Yeah, you cried when they wouldn't let you on last year," Harri said.

"Well … it wasn't fair," Kinga said, her bottom lip bagging.

"Let's do The Odyssey?" Harri pointed at a bright yellow ride that swooped and looped overhead. "It's 50.9 metres high, 891 metres long and has a 37.8-metre vertical loop, one of the biggest in Europe. It has five inversions. Five! And…" she said, like it was a good thing, "it has a max speed of at 62 miles per hour!"

As Jase watched, a carriage of people zipped by, hanging upside down. He swallowed again.

"How about we start on The Millennium?" Tyrone said, pointing at a pink ride not far away. "Ease ourselves into it all."

Jase liked the sound of easing. Easing was good.

"The Millennium is only 45.72 metres high with only two loops."

That didn't sound as bad as the others.

"But," she said, holding her finger up, "there is the Sidewinder."

"Oh, great," Jase said.

"Come on," Kinga said, looping her arm through his. "You're gonna love it!"

They waited in line for what felt like ages, before finally clambering into the seats of the roller coaster. The seat felt a bit sweaty from the last person. Or at least Jase hoped it was sweat. He pulled the restraints down as tight as he could, so tight they might be cutting off the circulation in his legs. The ride attendant checked everyone was in tight and then...

They were off.

Jase felt his heart thrown into the back of his chest. His stomach was suddenly where his lungs were meant to be. And he loved it.

It felt like soaring on a swing and travelling with your head stuck out a car window and learning to ride your bike for the first time all at once. By the time the ride came to an end (1 minute and 40 seconds later, according to Harri), Jase was beaming so much his cheeks hurt.

"Again!" he said.

They did every ride. Twice. Until they were too hungry and their legs too wobbly to do any more. So, they hit the marketplace to grab some food. There was so much to choose from, Jase didn't know where to start.

Tyrone made a beeline straight for Chicken By Chicken for some Jamaican food. "It's not as good as mine," he said, "but it's good enough."

Kinga was vegetarian so she hunted down a falafel stand, while Harri went for bubble waffles. Jase decided to stick to fish and chips.

They strolled along the seafront, eating their food. Jase struggled to finish his. His belly felt a bit churned up after all the rides.

"You don't want them?" Harri asked.

"They're all yours," Jase said, handing the remaining

chips to Harri. She finished them all, apart from a couple which she fed to the ravenous seagulls.

"Hang on," Tyrone said.

He'd stopped next to a game machine standing outside one of the arcades. It was one of those grabber machines, where you directed the arm to try to pick up prizes. It was filled with fluffy white sheep with hearts for eyes.

"Femi would love one of these," Tyrone said.

He pushed a coin into the slot and directed the arm towards one of the sheep. The hand came down and *stroked* the sheep, before returning to its place.

"Move over," Kinga said. "You're never any good on these."

Kinga cracked her knuckles and placed her hands on the joysticks like she was controlling a spaceship. With the tiniest of movements, she nudged the hand towards one of the fluffy sheep and hit the grab button. The hand zoomed down, plucked one of the sheep from the pile and dropped it into the shoot.

"There!" she said, handing the sheep to Tyrone.

"Thanks!" Tyrone said, pushing it into his hoodie pocket.

Jase noticed a group of kids heading straight for them. It was almost as if they were intentionally trying to get in their way.

They were mostly around Jase's age, apart from one boy who looked a few years older. He had blonde, spiky hair that was thick with hair gel, and he was wearing a yellow polo shirt, blue jeans that stopped just above his ankles and very white trainers. They looked expensive. So did the electric scooter he was riding on, though it had a scratch up the side.

He stopped the scooter right in front of Kinga.

"Hey, Kinga, were you dumped in a bin or what?" The boy had a posh accent that took Jase by surprise.

The boy looked around, waiting for the others to laugh at his joke. It took them a while to realize this was meant to be funny. When they did, they barked like seals.

"At least my parents chose me, Max," Kinga fired back. "Yours are stuck with you."

She sidestepped him and walked on, chin held high.

Max's blotchy cheeks went pale as he clenched his jaw. He clearly couldn't think of anything to say.

Harri snapped her fingers in the boy's face. "Told," she said.

Max finally found his voice. "Oh, Harriet, tell your brother we're looking for him."

Harri threw them a very rude sign.

Max zoomed off, his friends running after him.

"Who was that?" Jase said when he'd caught up with the others.

"That's Max," Tyrone said. "He's a local kid, and his parents are super rich so he seems to think the whole of Skegness belongs to him."

"And what was that about … a bin?" Jase asked.

"Oh, that's just Max being a loser," Kinga said. "I'm adopted and he seems to think that's something I would be embarrassed about."

"I'm sorry." Jase suddenly realized how that might have sounded. "I mean I'm sorry about what he said. Not that you were adopted," he said, flustered.

Kinga smiled. "That's OK. I know I won the lottery with my parents. I was born in Poland and my mum and dad adopted me when I was three. I don't remember my life before them, but they try to help me learn as much about my culture as possible. We're learning Polish together!"

"Your parents are the best," Harri said.

"Yeah, they're all right. Though I do wish they'd let

up a bit. Like, they're insisting they get me everything new for school when I don't need it. And we can't really afford it. I love them, but they're a little intense."

"Speaking of intense," Harri said, "who's up for The Volcano again?"

CHAPTER TWELVE

As they cycled back to Castle Rock, Jase still felt like he was on a roller coaster. Every time he closed his eyes, he could see the ground rushing up to meet him. So he tried not to close them too much.

They wound their way back through the site. As they passed Harri's caravan, they saw Mr Collins standing outside, along with Harri's parents and Guy.

Everyone looked VERY serious about something.

"Here she is," Mr Collins said, his mouth a stern line under his white moustache.

"What's going on?" Harri said, skidding her skateboard to a halt.

"We found THIS outside your bedroom window."

Mr Collins held something up and dangled it in their faces. It caught the sunlight and glinted.

A diamond earring.

"I've never seen that before," Harri said.

"It was STOLEN from Mrs McGinty," Mr Collins said, "along with a lot of other things."

"Hold on," Kinga said, stepping between Harri and the serious-looking adults. "I hope you're not accusing Harri of this? My dad's a solicitor; I know our rights."

She pressed her fists into her hips, as if daring them to take a step closer to her friend.

Tyrone too came to stand in front of Harri, though his posture was much calmer than Kinga's. "I'm sure there's been a misunderstanding," he said, holding his hands up as if trying to push away all the anger flying around.

"Look, mate," Harri's dad said to Mr Collins. Jase had never heard someone say "mate" with such force. "There is no way my Harri would go around nicking stuff."

"Yes," Harri's mum said. "Especially not earrings. She doesn't even have her ears pierced!"

Jase thought she was missing the point. It looked like a very expensive earring. If someone had stolen them, it wouldn't be to wear. It would be to sell.

Harri rolled her eyes at her mum's defence. She pushed everyone aside and stood in front of Mr Collins. They were about the same height.

"Search my room if you want," Harri said, pointing towards her caravan.

"I will do just that!" Mr Collins spun on his heels and stomped up caravan steps.

"What's all this here?" Jase turned at the familiar voice. It was his nana, striding towards them at top speed, Nicki and Sherlock trailing in her wake. When his nana wanted to be, she was as fast as Mo Farah.

"Nothing to do with you, madam," Mr Collins said, frozen to the spot.

"Madam?" Nana Rose said, pushing her shoulders back and lifting her chin. "MADAM? I'll have you know you're talking to Chief Constable Jackson of Nottinghamshire Police. Now, I asked you a question, sonny."

Sherlock gave a low, rumbling growl.

Mr Collins' red face went pale. He kept opening and closing his mouth like a fish.

Jase was caught between admiration for how brilliantly intimidating his nana could be and a squirming, bubbling fear that the dementia was really bad today. She often spoke about the old days. But she'd never forgotten that they WERE the old days.

"My mum was one of the best police detectives in the country, I'll have you know. Before she retired, right, Mum?" Nicki said, gently guiding her mother back to the present.

Nana Rose looked at her daughter for a moment and then smiled. "Well, yes, I am retired now. But I haven't forgotten the law. And this man is trying to enter a residence to do an illegal search." She pointed at him with one of her bony fingers.

Jase felt a wave of relief that he hadn't lost his nana quite yet. "He thinks my friend has stolen a diamond earring," he said.

"I see," Nana Rose said. "And what evidence does he have?"

"One of Mrs McGinty's earrings was found outside her window," Mr Collins said.

"Mabel McGinty would lose her head if it wasn't screwed on," Nana Rose said. "She probably just dropped it on her way to pick up the papers. If you notice, this is a direct line between her caravan and the store." She pointed in the direction of a caravan on the corner, then drew an imaginary line past where they were standing and over towards the store. "What thief would go to the effort of stealing the earrings only to be foolish enough to drop one?"

"That's as may be, but lots of things have been going missing," Mr Collins said.

"Well then. I can call my friends in the Skeggy nick and have this all done proper."

"Oh, we don't want to go to all that fuss. Police around the place will make my residents nervous."

"I really don't mind if he searches my room," Harri said. "I don't have anything to hide."

"If you're sure, love?" Nana Rose said, looking at Harri.

Harri nodded.

They all followed Mr Collins into the caravan. It was much smaller than Jase's caravan and it was a squeeze to fit them all inside. Guy took up most of the room on his own.

"Wha … what's going on?" Oliver emerged from his room. He looked at the people crowded in the caravan.

"Mr Collins thinks I'm the one who has been stealing from the site," Harri said.

Oliver's face flushed red. "But Harri would never. No way!"

He'd called her Harri, Jase noticed. It was kinda sweet the way he was ready to jump to her defence, no questions asked. He wasn't sure his brothers would be so quick to do the same for him. They'd probably have too much fun watching him squirm.

"Go on. Search away. My room is the one at the back," Harri said.

"Good luck finding anything in there," Harri's dad muttered.

"I told you, you should make her tidy it up," her mum said.

Mr Collins yanked the door open.

Jase peered past Guy's arm to look into the room. It was a mess of stuff. Clothes, shoes, another skateboard.

Comic books and drawing pads. Posters of space and rockets covered the walls.

Mr Collins stepped inside and started picking things up or prodding them with his foot.

After a while, they got bored watching him, and Harri's dad put the kettle on.

Finally, Mr Collins emerged. He wiped his hands on his shorts.

"Find anything?" Harri said. "Any missing watches or money or gnomes!"

"No."

"I think you owe this young lady an apology," Nana Rose said, bending down so her nose was an inch away from Mr Collins.

The man mumbled something.

"What was that?" Kinga said, pushing her phone into his face. "For the record."

His cheeks had gone bright red. "I didn't find anything. But don't think this is over. I will be keeping my eye on all of you, do you hear me? It might not have been her, but one of you in this room is the thief; I know it in my bones! One foot out of place and you'll be kicked off Castle Rock caravan site and banned for life!"

He pushed the adults aside and stormed out of the caravan.

They all followed him outside and watched him waddle away back to his office.

"Banned?" Kinga whispered.

"For life?" Tyrone added.

"But this is my happy place," Harri said. "It's the only place where we're all a family again." She sniffed back a tear.

Jase had only just arrived at Castle Rock. He didn't want to be kicked out. And what about his future as a detective? People branded as thieves didn't get to join the police. But he wasn't a thief, and neither were any of his friends. He was sure of it.

"There's only one thing for it then," he said.

All eyes turned to him.

"We'll have to work out who the real thief is!"

His nana smiled at him like she'd never been prouder.

CHAPTER THIRTEEN

In the morning, Jase scoffed down his cereal and was just about to leave when Nana Rose came out of her room.

She was always impeccably dressed. Even her pyjamas were pressed. And her hair was pinned up in a neat bun.

"Good morning," she said. "You're up bright and early."

"I wanted to get started on the investigation straight away! The early bird catches the thief and all."

"Oh, yes! Your jewellery thief," Nana said. "If you young'uns need any help, you just ask. The noggin's not what it was. But I reckon there's still enough rattling around in there to be of some help."

She tapped the side of her head and then gave his cheek a playful squeeze.

"Why are you all being so perky?" Nicki said, emerging from her room. Her hair was sticking up in all directions and she was wearing a baggy white T-shirt with a star on it and a pair of shorts.

"He's off to catch a criminal!" Nana Rose said.

"Huh?" Nicki was no good until she'd had at least two cups of tea in the morning.

"You know, finding the thief?" Jase said.

"Oh, sure. That." She flicked the kettle on. "Just don't get into trouble." Nicki stopped mid-pour and shook her head. "Forget that. Summer holidays are all about getting into trouble. Just don't get caught!"

Jase laughed. "I won't. See you later."

"Wait," Nana said. "You'll need this."

She pressed a small black notebook and a pen into his hands. "The first rule of investigating is you write down everything you hear or see, right?"

"Got it."

He gave his nana and auntie a quick kiss on their cheeks, whistled for Sherlock to follow, and headed out.

He met the others at the Gold Coast Arcade. They'd decided this would be their base in case it rained.

"Are we sure about this?" Tyrone said. "We're just kids."

"Don't you see?" Kinga said. "That's what makes us perfect! We can stick our noses into everything, and no one will think anything of it."

"Apart from Mr Collins, who is going to be watching us like a hawk," Harri said, still grumpy about being accused.

"Then we'll just have to stay out of his sight."

"We do know every inch of Castle Rock and practically everyone in it," Tyrone said.

"Exactly. And you can talk your way around anyone or anything," Kinga said.

"I do have a way with words," Tyrone said, a smile itching at the corner of his mouth.

"And Harri, you can hack your way into anything."

"Maybe I can get into Mr Collins' files!" Her eyes lit up at the idea.

"And my Google-fu is unparalleled," Kinga said, blowing on her painted fingernails. "All that researching I had to do for my exams has made me a pro. Plus, I'll capture all the evidence on my phone!" She waved her crystal-encrusted phone at them all.

Jase felt a sudden pang of panic. This had been his idea, but what could he offer? He was a little bit good at football. A little bit good at history. A little bit good at writing stories. But nothing compared to what the others could do.

"Maybe I could, I don't know, write stuff down?" He waved his notebook at them.

The other three looked at him like he was being dense.

"What are you talking about?" Tyrone said. "You're our lead detective!"

"Me?"

"Your nana was a detective, right?" Tyrone said.

"A badass chief constable in fact!" Kinga said.

Jase nodded.

"And she told you all her stories?" Tyrone added.

Jase nodded again.

"Well then," Kinga said. "We'll just do what she would have done!"

It was true that his nana had told him about being a detective so many times he felt like he'd been with her on those rainy stake-outs on the streets of Nottingham.

"I guess…" he said, feeling a bit more confident. "And Sherlock can help by sniffing stuff out."

Sherlock barked twice, excited to be involved.

"Great! Where do we start?" Tyrone asked.

Jase tried to remember his nana's stories. Usually, she focused on the dramatic endings. Chasing down the criminals and slapping them in cuffs. But how did they begin? Well, the detective shows they watched together always began in the same way. Nana said that was one of the things they got right.

"By interviewing the people who had their things stolen," Jase said. "Starting with Mrs McGinty. If we can work out why her earring ended up outside Harri's window, it might be a clue!"

Five minutes later, they were standing outside Mrs McGinty's caravan.

"You knock," Harri said.

"I don't think that's a good idea," Tyrone said. "She hasn't forgiven me for throwing my basketball into her geraniums last year."

"Well, she thinks I nicked her earring!"

"Oh, you two." Kinga moved them aside and knocked on the door.

There was the sound of shuffling and a few moments later, a woman opened the door. "Well?"

The woman was small and willowy thin, with long grey hair in a thick braid.

"We're here about your earrings," Kinga said.

"Have you found the matching one?"

"Afraid not," Kinga said. "But we had a few questions we wanted to ask you. You see, we're investigating the thefts."

"Are you now?" One of her thin eyebrows arched in apparent distrust. "Well, go on then."

Kinga grabbed Jase by the hand and yanked him forward. He cleared his throat nervously. "When was the last time you remember seeing your earrings?"

"I had them on Saturday night. I wore them to the karaoke night at the Clubhouse; I remember because Mandi Johal remarked on how nice they were."

"And you're certain you were still wearing them on your way home?" Kinga asked.

"Absolutely certain. I took them off before I went to sleep at 11 p.m. and left them on a dish by the bed."

"And you didn't see anyone around your caravan? Anyone suspicious?"

"Well, there's always kids zooming around here getting up to no good." She peered over Jase's head and gave Tyrone and Harri a dark glare.

"And did you see any of them near your caravan?" Jase said, writing everything down.

"No, I didn't."

"I think that's all we need for now," Jase said, flipping his notebook closed as he'd seen detectives do on TV shows. "Could you tell us where we could find Ms Johal?"

"She's in Sunflower, over there."

"Thank you, Mrs McGinty," Kinga said.

It was a similar story with Mandi Johal. She'd had twenty pounds stolen from her caravan on Saturday night. She'd left it in a bowl on the sideboard at 8.30 p.m. and it was gone when she'd got home from the pub at ten thirty.

The next person they spoke to was Mike Handley, the man who'd had his watch stolen while he was in the shower at 9 p.m. He too hadn't seen anyone unusual around on Saturday night.

The last person they spoke to was Ian Graves, the man with the gnomes.

"The watches and jewellery I get," Kinga said as they approached Mr Graves' caravan, "but why would anyone want to steal a gnome?"

"I don't know," Tyrone said. "That one is kinda cute."

He pointed at one of the bearded little men who had

a fishing pole thrown over his shoulder and a jaunty smile on his face.

They didn't need to knock. Mr Graves threw open the door. "Are you here about my gnome?" He sounded panicked, almost as if he thought he might be in trouble.

"Yes, sir," Jase said, settling into his role as lead detective. "We're here to ask you some questions."

Mr Graves folded his arms around his chest and told them everything he knew. The last time he'd seen his beloved gnome was on his way to the shops at 5.30 p.m. When he returned home at six it was gone.

"Gone! He was the pride of my collection. It doesn't look right without him."

They looked at the collection of gnomes. They just looked like little stone men to Jase. But the Crew reassured Mr Graves they would do everything they could to get his gnome back.

"What about there?" Jase said, pointing at the run-down camper van in the corner of the site. The one they'd skirted before.

"Oh no," Tyrone said. "Not there."

"Why not?" Jase said.

"We've never seen anyone in there during the day," Tyrone said.

"But we've heard noises at night," Kinga said.

"What kind of noises?"

Tyrone and Kinga shared a look.

"*Whhooooooo*," Kinga said, waving her arms around like she was a ghost.

"No, it's more of a '*grrrooooooooouuuggghhh*'," Tyrone said. "More like an animal."

"You're both ridiculous," Harri said, rolling her eyes.

"Well, you knock then!" Kinga said.

"I will!" Harri lifted her chin and walked towards the camper van. Jase followed, but Tyrone and Kinga stayed well back.

It was nearly midday and the sun was shining, but as they got closer to the van the shadows seemed to get darker. The air colder. Jase felt goosebumps break out over his arms and a cold clammy sweat prickled at the back of his neck.

Harri slowed, her confidence draining with every step.

Even Sherlock wasn't sure about this place. He made a low, rumbling growl.

Just as Kinga placed her foot on the bottom step, a sudden THUD made them all leap.

In the window, they saw a face. An eerie, skeletal face surrounded by dark shaggy fur, with black, sunken eyes. Eyes that were staring out at them.

"The bogeyman!" Harri screamed.

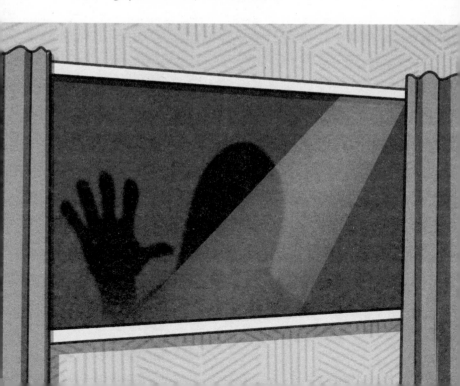

She turned and ran, nearly knocking Tyrone over. The others weren't far behind. They all ran away screaming and didn't stop till they got back to their caravans.

CHAPTER FOURTEEN

Jase slammed the door on his caravan and leaned against it, still panting. Sherlock ran and hid behind the settee.

When Jase's heart had stopped pounding, he risked peeking out the window to check the bogeyman hadn't followed him back.

"Boo!"

Jase nearly jumped out of his skin.

But it was only Nicki. She had snuck up behind him and pounced.

"You squeal like a mouse!" She laughed at Jase.

"You wouldn't be laughing if you'd seen what I've seen," Jase said.

"You mean your face?" Nicki teased. "You're lucky,

mate, you only see it when you pass a mirror. We have to look at it all day!"

He stuck his tongue out at her. "No, I mean the bogeyman."

"What bogeyman?" Nana Rose said. She was sitting on the settee watching with amusement, a magazine open on her lap.

"The one in the camper van on the far side of the site. The one all on its own. There's a bogeyman in there!"

"Not the notorious bogeyman of Castle Rock? The one who gobbles up little boys whole?" Nicki pounced on Jase again and tickled his belly with wriggling hands.

He tried not to giggle. "Geroff," he said, pushing her away.

Back in the safety of his caravan, he didn't feel so scared of the creepy camper van or the face they'd seen in the window.

"What have you been doing messing around there?"

"We thought there might be a clue to our investigation," Jase said.

"Hmmm," his nana said. "Now that you mention

it, I don't know who's living in the van."

"Well, I'm not sure anyone in there is *living*!" Jase said. "I think he might be a ghost."

"Nonsense," Nana Rose said with a snort.

"That's what Harri said. Then she saw the face. She screamed loudest of all."

"If you're going to be a police detective, Jase, you have to focus on facts. What have you learned so far?" She put the magazine aside and crossed her legs.

Jase pulled out his notebook.

"Well, so far we know that all the thefts happened on Saturday night."

"And where and when exactly did they happen?"

Jase checked his notes. "Um, from all over. Mrs McGinty had her earrings stolen from her caravan sometime after 11 p.m. when she took them off to go to bed. Mr Handley had his watch taken while he was in the shower at 9 p.m. Miss Johal had her twenty pounds taken after 8.30 p.m., when she left to go to the karaoke night. And Mr Graves' gnome was taken from outside his caravan between 5.30 and 6 p.m. And then there's my birthday coin and Kinga's camera. And Harri's Switch. All taken from our caravans on Saturday night."

"And no sign of any break–ins?"

"No, no damage at all. Just the missing things."

"Hmmm, then your thief is probably a master of lockpicks."

Jase hadn't thought of that. He wrote it down in his notebook to tell the others.

"Hang on." Nana Rose pushed herself up out of her seat with an *ooff* and walked over to the sideboard. She pulled open drawers, digging around inside for something.

"What's she looking for?" Nicki asked.

Jase shrugged.

"Here we are!" Nana Rose said triumphantly, waving something over her head.

She brought it back to the coffee table and unfolded it. It was a large map. A map of Castle Rock.

Jase and Nicki leaned over it. It was old. The title read "Welcome to Castle Rock 1992". And yet it still had the same road names and all the caravan sites marked in neat white boxes.

"There was this arson case I worked on when I was first starting out as a detective," Nana Rose said, smoothing out the creases. "One summer, someone was setting fire to bins around the city."

"Bins?" Jase said.

"Yup. These fires were popping up all over the place, so at first they thought there might be a group of people doing it. But then I mapped out every bin location and worked out they were all on the 35B bus route. The firebug was hopping on and off the buses to start the fires. So, all I had to do was ride the 35B for a day and I got 'em!"

"Amazing!" Jase said.

"Turns out it was a waste collector who had been fired by the council and wanted to get his own back."

"That's incredible, Mum, but what does it have to do with Jase's thefts?" Nicki asked.

Nana Rose didn't answer straight away. She was scanning the room, looking for something. Jase followed the laser track of her stare, trying to see what she was seeing.

"That!" she said at last, pointing to a framed picture of a couple dancing on a beach in the rain.

She reached up and unhooked the frame from the wall. Jase breathed in. Was there something hiding behind the picture? A wall safe? A hidden camera?

Nana Rose turned the picture around and then hung it back up by its string, the brown corkboard side facing out.

"Huh?" Nicki said, expressing what Jase was feeling.

"Where's my sewing kit?" Nana Rose asked.

Nicki dug around in one of the cupboards and brought out a wooden box with a padded lid. Multi-coloured pins stuck out of the lid like a mutant hedgehog.

"Perfect!" Nana said as Nicki placed the box next to her.

Using the pins, she stuck the map to the back of the picture and then stood back.

Finally, Jase understood what was going on. "An evidence board!"

"Exactly!" Nana Rose said. "So, Mabel's caravan is here." Nana Rose prodded at the spot on the map with her finger. "Go on, pin it!"

Jase grabbed one of the pins from the box and pushed it into the spot.

Nana Rose then opened the lid of the sewing box and pulled out a ball of purple wool. "Red looks better," she said. "But this will do."

She unwound a line of the wool and snipped it when it was about thirty centimetres long. She then wrapped it around the head of the pin and pinned the other end to one side of the board.

Jase was already ahead of her. He grabbed his pen and did a very bad drawing of Mrs McGinty and a pair of diamond earrings (he'd get Kinga to do a better one later) on pages in his notebook. He pinned these clues next to the end of the string.

"And mark the time. It's essential we build an accurate timeline."

On another scrap of paper, Jase wrote "11 p.m. – 7 a.m." followed by three question marks and pinned

it next to the clues about Mrs McGinty.

"And Ian Graves and his ugly gnomes are here." His nana prodded another spot on the map.

Jase pinned that spot too and added a new line of the wool leading to a picture of Mr Graves, his gnome and "5.30 p.m. – 6 p.m.".

"And Miss Johal lives here." He circled another spot. "And Mr Handley's … here."

Jase put a pin in each place and attached the related clues.

"Do you see a pattern? When working on any investigation, we're always looking for patterns."

Jase took a few steps back and looked at the pins and threads marked. They were dotted around the caravan site with no apparent connection. Then he saw something. He grabbed the wool and started wrapping it from pin to pin, connecting the dots. It made a perfect circle. And right at the centre…

"Isn't that your friend Harri's caravan?" Nicki asked. "The girl with the cool hair?"

Jase nodded. He had a feeling like lead in his belly.

"And you're absolutely sure it wasn't her?" Nana said.

"Absolutely!" Jase said quickly.

"What exact proof do you have?" his nana asked, looking at him down her long nose.

"Well … I don't…" He realized he didn't actually have any proof it wasn't Harri other than her word. And now that his nana mentioned it, hadn't Harri said she couldn't afford to buy her dad a birthday present? What if she *had* stolen the things to get the money for him?

He looked at the other caravans inside the circle. Tyrone's was there. And Kinga's too. Could it have been them?

Tyrone had said he would do anything to be able to afford a new pair of trainers. And then Kinga, she'd said she was worried about not having the money for school stuff.

Any of his new friends could be the thief!

"It's OK," Nana Rose said, seeing the anxiety creeping across Jase's face. "I don't think it's any of your friends, either."

"But how can you be sure?" Jase said, a panicked

whine to his voice.

His nana rested her hand on his shoulder. "You know the most important tool a police detective will ever have?"

"Umm, your badge?" Jase said.

"Your handcuffs?" Nicki said, joining in.

"No. Your gut!" Nana Rose slapped her belly. "You gotta learn to trust your gut. You can have all the facts and information in the world, but it's your gut that will lead you right every time."

Jase looked down at his stomach. Right now, his gut wasn't telling him anything other than the fact that he was hungry. All this detecting had been hard work.

"Come on," Nicki said, taking the ball of wool out of Jase's hands. "You can solve the great mystery of Castle Rock tomorrow. Let's go get lunch."

Jase looked back at the evidence board. He'd show it to the others tomorrow. Maybe one of them would see what he wasn't seeing. He just hoped he wasn't going to discover that one of his friends really was behind the thefts.

CHAPTER FIFTEEN

Jase woke early the next day to a ping from his phone. Groggily, he reached for it and saw the screen was full of notifications.

He'd been added to a chat group called "Castle Rock Crew". The messages had been blowing up his phone all night. Most of them from Harri.

Harri: You lot awake? 👀

Harri: Hellooooo? 👋

Harri: I can't sleep.

Harri: I can't believe Mr Collins thought I was behind the thefts. The cheek of it!

Harri: Who do you think it was?

Harri: We have to find them!! 🔍

Tyrone: It's 2 am. Go to sleep. zᶻᶻ We'll keep on looking in the morning.

Harri: I think best at night. 🖥️

Harri: It's the quiet. My brain goes into overdrive. 🤓🤓🤓

Harri: You know, I think that Mrs McGinty might know more than she's letting on. 🤔

Harri: Or it could be Max or one of the other townie kids?

Harri: What do you think?

Kinga: Stop hyperfixating. Write all your thoughts down and we'll read them together.

IN THE MORNING!!!

Harri: That's exactly what I'm doing! I'm writing them all down. ✍️

Harri: Here in this chat.

Tyrone has left the group chat.
Kinga has left the group chat.

Harri: RUDE!!!
Harri: Just you and me then, Jase.
Harri: Jase, are you awake?
Harri: Jase?
Harri: Hello? Jase!!!

Harri had finally stopped texting at 4.15 a.m. Jase felt guilty because he had slept through all of her messages.

The most recent message, the one which had woken him, was from Tyrone.

Tyrone: Morning! We're meeting at the Coast after 🔍.

Jase fired back a response.

See you there.

He gave the clothes he'd been wearing a quick sniff. They didn't smell too bad. He pulled them back on again and went into the living room. His nana and Nicki were already up, though Nicki only looked half awake. She was nursing a cup of tea like it was her best friend.

"Sleep well, kid?" she said.

"Yeah, not bad!"

"Morning, Nana!"

"Oh, morning…" his nana said. She looked a bit sleepy too.

He poured milk over cereal and shovelled it into his mouth as quickly as he could.

"You will choke on that one day," Nicki said.

Jase drank the last drips of milk from his bowl and wiped his chin.

"OK if I head straight out to meet my friends? We're continuing with the investigation."

"What investigation is that, love?" his nana asked.

"The thefts!" Jase said excitedly. "You know, from

the camp site?" His enthusiasm drained away as he realized the sparkle in his nana's eyes wasn't shining as bright this morning. And she'd been so THERE just the night before.

Sometimes it felt like she was a radio picking up a frequency. Some days the frequency was loud and clear. Other times it crackled. Today was a crackly day.

"Oh, yes, the thefts," she said, sounding unsure.

"She didn't sleep that well last night," Nicki said quietly. She took his empty bowl off him and put it in the sink. "I think we'll take it easy today. I might just take her for a walk on the beach."

"Do you want me to stay?"

Nicki kissed him on the top of his head. "You're all right, love. You go have fun."

Jase hesitated before leaving.

Nicki made a shooing motion. "Get on with you. You'll only get under our feet here."

He turned to Sherlock. "You coming?"

Sherlock made a small *rwuff* and moved to sit by Nana Rose's feet. She gave him a gentle pat on his head.

"Good boy," Jase said. At least he knew Sherlock would be there to look after them.

He'd make it up to Nicki and Nana Rose later. First, he had a crime to solve.

He unhooked the evidence board from the wall. It was too large to carry under one arm, so he held it out in front of him, hoping the scraps of paper wouldn't blow away.

Harri and Kinga were arguing when Jase arrived at the Coast.

Harri was waving her arms around. Her brightly coloured hair wasn't up in its usual buns, and she looked a bit wild.

"But it makes perfect sense!" Harri said.

"Beryl?" Kinga said. "Old Beryl! Come off it, Harri. You'll be saying it was one of the gnomes next."

"It's always the last person you expect. And who is the last person we expect!"

"What's going on?" Jase asked Tyrone, placing the board down on the snooker table.

"Harri has been working her way through every

suspect on the site. So far, she's said it was Mrs McGinty, stealing her own earrings for the insurance. Mr Collins because for some reason he wants the site shut down. And now it's Beryl."

Jase laughed.

"Well, who do you think it is then?" Harri asked, turning on him.

"I … I don't know. But I think I have a place to start. My nana and I…" He stopped for a second. A stab of guilt for not being with his nana twisted in his gut. But Nicki was right. He wouldn't be much help. "My nana and I marked up where and when all the thefts happened. She said the job of a detective is to look for patterns."

He propped the evidence board up against the wall and talked them through each bit of evidence.

"Is that meant to be me?" Kinga asked, peering at the scribble of her. "You're a good detective, Jase, but a terrible artist! Let me have a go."

Kinga drew better versions of Jase's scribbled stickmen and pinned them in place.

"And that's my caravan bang in the middle," Harri said miserably.

"But don't you see? We have proof it wasn't you!" Kinga said, beaming.

"We do?" Harri said.

"Yes! The gnome was taken around 6 p.m. on Saturday night, right?" She pointed to the cluster of clues around Mr Graves. "Well, at 6 p.m. you were here. Playing that! And we were all witnesses."

She ran over to the racing game, pointing at the top scores screen where the letters HRI were flashing at the top.

"All three of us can vouch for you," Jase said.

"And I bet if I was able to get into the code of the game, I could even find time data attached to the score," Harri said, looking around the back of the machine to see if there was a way in.

"And parents say video games are a waste of time!" Tyrone said.

Jase saw something glint out of the corner of his eye. Something from the coin pusher machine.

He walked over and peered through the smudged glass. He wiped at the glass with the cuff of his sleeve. There, among the piles of coins was one different to all the others. It was slightly bigger and had One Penny written around the top.

"It's my coin!" he shouted.

The others ran over.

"Where?"

"There." He prodded the glass above his birthday coin. It was right on the edge. One push in the right place and it would topple over.

"Anyone got a 2p?" he asked.

"No need," Harri said. "Stand back."

She ran her hand along the side of the machine. Then gave it a thump.

His coin jumped up in the air and toppled over, pouring out into the tray, along with a handful of other coins.

He retrieved it. "You're a genius, Harri!"

"It's been said."

"Did you put it in there by mistake?" Tyrone said.

"No! I've never played the game."

"It wasn't there yesterday," Harri said.

"Which means…" Kinga said.

"The thief must have been in here this morning!" Tyrone said.

Jase ran his thumb over the coin. He was relieved to have it back and he wasn't going to lose it again. He put it in his front jean pocket, the tiny one he'd never used before.

"They must have stolen the coin from my caravan," he said. "But not known that it was a special coin and used it in the machine!"

They all looked at each other. They had their first concrete clue!

"Let me!" Kinga said, grabbing the notepad. She drew a picture of the coin machine and pinned it on the board.

"But … how can we work out who was here this morning?"

They looked around. The Coast was empty apart from them.

"There!" Harri pointed at something on the ceiling.

"What?"

"A CCTV camera! If we can look at the footage, we can see who was in here!"

"But Mr Collins is never going to let us," Tyrone said.

"No need." Harri ran back over to the pool table and threw her rucksack on it. She unzipped it and pulled out a laptop. It was covered in stickers of all kinds.

She flung it open. "The CCTV will be on a local network, so I just need to find the IP address."

"Can you seriously do that?" Kinga asked, sounding amazed.

"Sure. I did it at school to prove that the teachers were vaping in the teachers' lounge."

Jase watched open-mouthed as Kinga opened a black screen and began typing. Numbers scrolled past.

"There. Got the IP address. Now I just need to run a password hacker to log in…"

Harri's fingers flew across the keyboard.

"Harri, remind me never to get on the wrong side of you," Tyrone said.

A moment later, she punched the air. "And we're in!"

It had taken a matter of minutes and Harri had access to the CCTV footage for the last twenty-four hours.

Jase was pretty sure what Harri had done wasn't strictly legal. But it was for a good cause.

They could see themselves as viewed through the camera lens. The colours were muted. Instead of smooth footage, the image came through in a series of disjointed stills, almost like watching someone flip through a flick book. It was kinda dizzying.

"Why is it so jerky?" Jase asked.

"Slow frame rate to save memory," Harri said.

Jase didn't know what that meant. But he shrugged.

"Scroll back a couple of hours," Kinga said.

Harri rewound the footage until before any of them had arrived at The Gold Coast.

"Stop."

They watched someone walk into the room. Just five minutes before they had. Oliver, Harri's brother. He played on the 2p machine for a minute before leaving.

"You don't think…?" Kinga said.

Harri shook her head. "He was in the caravan when I got home, and Mr Graves says his gnome was taken just before 6 p.m. So Oliver doesn't fit the timeline."

"Hmmm. Can you go back further?" Jase asked.

She did. A second figure appeared and walked over to the pusher machines. They were tall, so maybe a man. The group leaned in closer. Here was their thief! But ... they couldn't see their face because they were holding a huge pink fluffy rabbit next to their head.

It was one of the biggest toys Jase had ever seen, the kind you won on the arcades if you were really good.

"Gotcha!" Kinga said.

The others looked at her. Got who? Who had they got?

"Don't you see?" she said. None of them did. "All we have to do is follow the pink rabbit and we'll find our thief!"

CHAPTER SIXTEEN

"Let's split up," Tyrone said. "We can cover more ground that way. Kinga and Harri, you take the south."

"On it." Harri and Kinga high-fived.

"Jase, we'll take the north. Anyone sees anything, you text, OK?"

"Great! But what do we do with that?" Kinga said, pointing at the evidence board.

She was right. They couldn't just leave it lying around. Then Jase had an idea.

He flipped the board over, revealing the painting on the other side, and hooked it on a nail sticking out of the wall.

"Brilliant!" Kinga said. "No one will suspect anything."

"Let's go," Jase said, charging out of the arcade.

Before they went in separate directions, they pulled off the Castle Rock Crew handshake. Jase almost had it down perfectly. Almost.

Kinga and Harri raced off towards the seafront while Jase followed Tyrone towards the site exit.

They scanned every window and doorway, looking for any glimpse of the pink rabbit.

When Jase had imagined hunting down criminals, he'd pictured large angry men with snarling attack dogs. Or criminal masterminds with sharp suits and fluffy white cats. Pink rabbits hadn't featured all that much. He wondered if Nana Rose had ever followed a fluffy toy on one of her cases.

One thing his nana had talked about a lot was the thrill of the chase. And he was starting to understand why. His heart was pounding in his chest, and it wasn't just because he was running so fast to keep up with Tyrone. He felt giddy with the adrenaline. They were on a hunt for a criminal, just like he'd always dreamed. As his feet pounded on the gravel drives of Castle Rock, he imagined his face on the front cover of the local newspapers. Tyrone, Harri and Kinga by his side. He could even see the headline: **KID DETECTIVES TAKE DOWN MASTER THIEF**.

Maybe they'd even get an award?

Suddenly, Jase saw a flash of pink disappearing between two caravans. "There!" he shouted.

He and Tyrone put on a burst of speed. When they reached the caravans, they saw Mr Graves. He was wearing a bright pink T-shirt, but there was no rabbit in sight.

Mr Graves jumped when he saw them and dropped the spade he had been using to dig a hole.

"Oh, it's you!" he said, clutching at his chest. "I was just … just…" He looked down at the hole. "Gardening?"

"Got to go!" Tyrone said. "Pink rabbit to find." He waved cheerily, and they ran off.

Jase looked back over his shoulder at Mr Graves,

who had returned to his digging. Gardening? Why
would anyone want to garden BEHIND their caravan?
Another mystery for another day.

Jase followed Tyrone up and down the rows of
caravans, ducking down the cul-de-sacs, jumping over
fences and squeezing down alleyways. Tyrone seemed
to know every shortcut on the site.

Every now and then, they'd be sure they'd spotted it.
But it would turn out to be a beach towel or a balloon.
And in one case, a kid holding a massive ball of candy
floss. But no rabbits.

They'd covered the whole of the north of the site and were almost about to give up when they reached Mr Collins' office.

It was a small, converted caravan with a sign saying "Site Manager" pinned to the wall. And there, in the window, was a huge pink fluffy toy.

Jase and Tyrone traded looks. Had the site owner really been behind it all along?

They slowed as they approached. They could see Mr Collins moving around inside. They got closer, close enough that they could hear him shouting at someone on the phone.

"If I knew where it was, I wouldn't be calling you now, would I?"

There was another pause as he waited for an answer.

"OK. Good. And listen, this stays between me and you, OK? If anyone finds out about the skeleton key, I'm done for."

"What's a skeleton key?" Jase whispered. He imagined a key made of bones. It made his skin go clammy.

Tyrone shrugged. "I don't know, but he's up to

something!" Tyrone laid his hand on the door handle and had just thrown the door open dramatically when Jase grabbed his arm.

"Wait!" Jase said. "It's an elephant!"

"What?" Tyrone said, his brow wrinkled in confusion.

"Look. The toy. It's an elephant. Not a rabbit."

Now they were up close, they could see that, yes, the fluffy toy in the window had a trunk and large round ears. It also looked as if it had been sitting in the window for years. It had once been red, judging by the colour of the tail, but had faded to pink in the sun. And the orange bow around its neck had gone the colour of weak tea.

"What do you two want?" Mr Collins said, putting the phone to his chest so whoever was on the other end couldn't hear what was going on.

"Nothing!" Tyrone said.

"Sorry. Wrong place," Jase said, retracing their steps away from the office.

"Phew!" Tyrone said when they were in the clear.

"Can you imagine what he'd have done if we'd accused him?"

"Told us to make like an elephant?"

Tyrone tilted his head, not following.

"And pack our trunks?" Jase explained.

"Trunks!" Tyrone burst out laughing.

Jase started laughing too. Mostly from relief at not having been kicked off the site.

Jase jumped as his phone buzzed in his pocket. He still wasn't used to getting texts. He pulled it out.

Kinga: We've found it!

Tyrone replied before Jase could.

Tyrone: Where?

Harri: The pub!

Tyrone: We'll be there in five!

They made it to the pub in three minutes.

Harri and Kinga were hiding behind a bush.

"Pssst!" Harri hissed.

Tyrone and Jase ducked down and joined them behind the shrubbery.

The pub was called The Jolly Fisherman. Outside hung a sign of a man wearing a bright yellow raincoat and holding a large fish. The windows were covered with a frosted film so people couldn't see inside.

"We saw someone carrying a pink rabbit in there!" Kinga whispered.

"Who was it?" Jase asked.

"We're not sure," Harri said. "They were too far in the distance."

"And you're sure it wasn't an elephant?" Jase said.

"Huh?" Kinga and Harri said at the same time.

"I'll tell ya later."

"Then why are we hiding?" Tyrone said, standing up.

He strode over to the door of the pub. The others followed at a distance.

Tyrone pulled open the door, turned around to smile at the others, and walked straight into what could have been a brick wall, but was a woman.

"Where do you think you're going, love?" she said. She was wearing a black bomber jacket, a pair of black leggings and flip-flops. Her toenails were painted bright yellow.

"Um, inside?" Tyrone said weakly.

"No kids without an accompanying adult," the bouncer said.

"We just want a very quick look," Kinga said. "We won't even sit down."

The bouncer sniffed. "I don't make the rules, love, I just enforce 'em. Now, why don't you run off to the soft play area?"

"Soft play?" Harri said, offended. "How old do you think we are?"

The bouncer sniffed again and looked them up and down. "Six?"

"Six?!"

"I don't know, do I? But I know you're too young to be coming in here. Now, do one." She gestured with her thumb for them to move it and closed the door again.

"What are we going to do now?" Kinga said.

"We could wait till whoever's in there comes out?" Jase said.

"Yes! Like a stake-out!" Tyrone said.

"That could take all day!" Kinga said. "And I told my parents I'd go to the seal sanctuary."

"Aww, jealous. The seals are so cute!" Tyrone said.

"Focus, you lot. We have to get in there," Harri said, stamping her foot.

"But you heard the bouncer. No kids," Tyrone said.

They stared at the door to the pub as if they could wish it away.

"Maybe I could ask my parents?" Kinga said. "Only, then they'd want to be involved in everything and that would be a nightmare!"

"We could sneak in through the loo window?" Harri suggested.

"I have an idea," Jase said, a little uncertainly. He'd seen it in a film, but it might just work.

"Excellent! What is it?" Tyrone said.

"Can any of you get your hands on a trench coat?"

CHAPTER SEVENTEEN

Tyrone returned minutes later with a trench coat that belonged to one of his uncles. It was massive.

"I brought a hat, too!" Tyrone said, waving both triumphantly. The hat had a small feather tucked into the ribbon around the brim.

"Perfect!" Jase said.

"Two kids under a trench coat," Harri said, almost wistfully. "Classic."

As soon as Jase had explained his plan, the others had got behind it instantly.

"The question is," Kinga said, "which two kids?"

The four all looked at each other, waiting to see who would be the first to volunteer.

"Well my coordination is rubbish!" Harri said with a shrug. "I'd only fall over and ruin everything."

Harri was great on a skateboard or behind the wheel of a racing game, but Jase had noticed that when just walking around, she did tend to bump into things a lot. So, she was probably right.

"Well, it's my idea," Jase said, "so I'm definitely in."

That left one more.

"You and me, Tyrone?" Jase asked. "You can go on my shoulders."

Tyrone looked suddenly anxious. He glanced over to the pub door and back to the group. "She'll probably remember my face. Besides, one man with Black arms and White legs, might be a giveaway." He forced a smile.

Tyrone seemed so confident. But when it came to actually getting into trouble, he seemed to lose his cool. Jase wondered if it had to do with having such a big family who could all shout at him. It wasn't as if *he* liked getting into trouble, but he knew that Nicki would probably find it all hilarious and his nana would understand the lengths you had to go to for a case. Just so long as his mum never found out, he would be OK.

"I'll do it!" Kinga said. "I'm the smallest anyway."

Kinga wrapped her hair into a bun and pulled on the trench coat. It fell far past her fingers and pooled on the floor around her feet. With a lot of effort and the help of a nearby lamp post, she clambered up on to Jase's shoulders.

Tyrone and Harri buttoned the coat up, leaving one button open halfway down so Jase could see where he was going. Kinga put her sunglasses on and held her hands out.

"Whaddya reckon?"

"All you need is..." Tyrone stretched up on his tiptoes and placed the hat on Kinga's head.

"Take a picture! Take a picture!" Kinga said, handing her phone down to Harri.

She posed, hands on her hips, while Jase staggered around, trying not to fall over.

Photo taken, Harri handed the phone back.

"Right, let's go!" Kinga pointed ahead, like a captain on the prow of a ship.

Jase took a first unsteady step forward and then another. The other two ducked back behind the bush and watched.

Kinga swung the long sleeves of the trench coat back and forth as if they were a perfectly normal, if rather tall, human going for a walk on a summer's day. Wearing a trench coat, sunglasses and a hat.

Jase was having serious second thoughts. When he'd seen this in the film, he hadn't thought about carrying the weight of another person on his shoulders.

"Try to look casual," Kinga said.

"I'm trying!" Jase replied.

Wobbling step after wobbling step, they reached the door of the pub. Kinga pushed it open and they stepped inside. The bouncer was sitting on a stool by the door reading a comic book. She didn't glance up so they kept going.

Jase could only see a little through the tiny gap in the coat. He could see the bar and the TV screens behind it showing a football match. And a barmaid with thick red hair pulled into a tight bun right on the top of her head. She was up a ladder cleaning the bottles on the bar and hadn't noticed them yet.

He was starting to feel a little claustrophobic inside the trench coat. It smelled of mothballs and he could feel a sneeze itching at his nose.

"Move forward," Kinga hissed. "I think I see something."

Jase took a lurching step forward. There, on the bar, was a large, pink fluffy rabbit. It was sitting facing out, a big happy grin on its whiskered face. It was one of the rabbits you could win down at Fantasy Island. But who had won it and, more importantly, who had brought it here?

"Oh my, what a distinguished-looking rabbit," Kinga said in a deep old-man's voice. "Wherever did you get it?"

"Thanks," the barmaid said. "It was a gift for my daughter from—"

Before she could say who had given her the rabbit, Jase felt something tugging on the trench coat.

"Oi!"

Slowly, Jase turned around to face the bouncer. She looked them up and down.

"Hello, my good lady!" Kinga said in her old-man voice. "May we trouble you for a pint of ale?"

The bouncer reached up and plucked the hat and glasses off Kinga's face.

"You again," she said with a snarl. "And my, you seem to have grown."

"I have no idea what you mean. This is my first time in this fine establishment!" Kinga said, keeping up the deep voice, despite having been caught.

It was then that Jase lost the fight with the sneeze. It was one of those huge, *Ahhh, ahhhh, choooo* spluttering sneezes.

The bouncer pulled open the trench coat in the middle to reveal Jase's face. He grinned sheepishly and waved. Then wiped his nose with the back of his sleeve.

"All right, you two. Sling your hooks before I tell your parents."

The bouncer grabbed the sleeve of the trench coat and dragged them out. Kinga protested the whole time, but Jase was glad it was over. His shoulders were aching, and the smell of mothballs was making his eyes water.

"Well, I will be sure to tell my friends not to frequent this public house," Kinga said, still in character.

The bouncer chucked the hat and sunglasses out after them and slammed the door.

Jase bent down so Kinga could get off his shoulders. It was a relief to be able to stand properly again. Kinga was only light, but it had still been hard work.

The other two ran out from behind the bushes.

"What happened?" Tyrone said.

"We found the pink rabbit," Kinga said.

"But we got caught," Jase added, disappointed.

All that effort and they had only been inside for less than a minute. And they hadn't found out the identity of the person carrying the rabbit.

"It doesn't matter," Kinga said, slapping Jase on the shoulder with a flappy trench coat sleeve. "I filmed everything!" She pushed back her sleeve to reveal her phone. "Now we just need to check the footage." Kinga shrugged the trench coat off and strode off happily. "Why, what a glorious day we are having," she said, still in her old-man voice.

Jase had to give it to the girl: she committed to a role.

On their way back to the Coast, they stopped at the shop to grab drinks and snacks. In all the excitement, they'd forgotten to have lunch. Now, they were huddled around Kinga's phone watching the footage, while shovelling crisps into their mouths. It was shaky from all the wobbling, but they could make out two other people in the pub.

The first was old Beryl. She was sitting at the bar, sipping a red drink from a small glass and reading a newspaper. Every now and then, she'd pluck a small pencil from behind her ear, scribble notes on the paper, then tuck it behind her ear again. She had looked up at Kinga's phone and grinned, then returned to her newspaper.

"You don't think…" Kinga said.

"Nah," Tyrone said. "She's too old to be a thief."

Jase wasn't sure about that. Plenty of his nana's stories involved old people. But for some reason, he couldn't imagine Beryl walking around with the pink rabbit.

"What about him?" Harri said as the camera panned around the pub.

Sitting by a table in the corner was a man with a shaggy beard. He was wearing a baggy jumper with holes in it and was drinking a cup of tea and staring out the window.

"I know that face!" Jase said.

He wracked his brain, trying to remember where he'd seen it before.

"He definitely looks familiar," Harri said. "But I don't think I've seen him on the site."

Jase closed his eyes, trying to match the face of the man in the bar with anyone he'd seen since he arrived at Castle Rock.

Think, Jase said to himself. *Think*.

And then he remembered. He had seen that face staring out at them from the spooky camper van. The same face that had scared them all half to death.

"It's the bogeyman!"

CHAPTER EIGHTEEN

They agreed to meet at midnight at the bogeyman's camper van.

It was 11.30 p.m. Jase lay in bed, fully dressed, with the duvet pulled up to his neck just in case Nicki came in to check on him. He listened to the sounds of the caravan. His nana had gone to bed at nine, but Nicki had been up watching TV until eleven fifteen. He'd been worried she'd still be up when he was due to leave, but at last, she'd turned the TV off and gone to bed. The only thing he could hear now was Sherlock snoring from the settee in the living room and the creaks and groans of the caravan settling. Everything sounded so much louder at night.

He checked his watch for the hundredth time. Eleven fifty. It was now or never.

He'd never snuck out at night before. His heart pounded in his ears as he slipped his trainers on and opened the door as slowly and quietly as he could.

Sherlock opened an eye as he tiptoed past.

"Shush," he said, holding a finger up to his mouth.

Sherlock yawned and went back to sleep.

Jase's hand was on the door handle when he heard a cough behind him.

"And where do you think you're off to?"

He turned to see his nana standing there, her arms folded across her chest. Busted.

"I ... I was just…" There was no point in lying. Not to his nana. She always knew when he wasn't telling the truth.

"It's for the investigation, Nana. We're having a stake-out."

She sniffed. Jase heard the ticking of the clock on the sideboard. Was she going to stop him? Shout at him?

"Well, in that case…" she said at last. "You'll

need this."

She opened one of the drawers in the cabinet and pulled out a large black torch.

Jase took it and slipped it into his rucksack.

"Thanks, Nana," he said.

"And if Nicki asks where you are, I'll blame the dementia and say I forgot." She winked at him.

Jase gave his nana a hug and then hurried outside.

Tyrone was waiting for him by his caravan. His skin had a green tinge, as if he might be sick.

"If my mum or dad catch me," Tyrone said, "I'm dead."

"You don't have to come," Jase said.

"No," Tyrone said quickly. "I'm not gonna let you lot sneak around alone. Someone has to be there to stop you doing anything dangerous. Well, anything more dangerous than what we're already doing."

Jase grinned. "Come on then."

Before they could leave, they heard the creaking of the door. Jase ducked down out of sight, but Tyrone froze in the beam of light coming from the door.

"Ty? Where are you going?"

It was Femi. She was dressed in a long T-shirt with a picture of a puppy on it and was dragging the sheep Kinga had won her by its leg. She yawned. She must have just woken up.

Tyrone ran back to his little sister. "Go back to bed, Femi," he whispered. "I'll be back soon."

"I wanna come."

"You can't. We're on a secret mission."

"Secret?" Femi said, rubbing at her eyes.

"Yes, and if you help me keep the secret, I will get you an even bigger toy than that one."

She hugged the sheep to her chest. "Even bigger?"

"Even bigger! But you have to go back to bed and don't tell anyone!"

"OK," she said.

She turned and stumbled back inside, dragging the sheep behind her.

Tyrone let out a long sigh. "That was close."

"Too close," Jase said. "Let's get a move on."

They met the others by the camper van. It looked

even spookier at night. The low orange glow from the street light only seemed to make the shadows darker. Moss grew up the sides. And the curtains covering the windows were so moth-eaten they looked like old, grubby lace.

"There's no one in there," Kinga said after they'd been watching the place for ten minutes. She was wearing a new sweatshirt with a seal on the front, which she'd got from the seal sanctuary. Jase was only wearing a T-shirt. He was starting to get cold.

"Prob best we call it a night, then," Tyrone said; he was also dressed in light clothes.

"The window's open," Harri said.

Jase hadn't noticed it before, but Harri was right. One of the windows was open just a crack.

"Why don't we have a quick look around?" Harri said.

"What?" Tyrone said. "Go inside?"

"Well, he's not in, is he? There's no sound, no lights. He must be out. Just a quick in and out to see if we can see any of the stolen stuff around?" Harri said.

Jase wasn't thrilled about breaking into someone's

home. But he was certain this man was their thief. Maybe if they were really quick?

"OK, let's do it!"

Jase and Harri crept forward, listening out for the faintest sound of movement. Kinga followed behind them, while Tyrone hovered at the back.

"Are you coming?" Jase whispered back to him.

"I … I don't want to get my Jordans scuffed up."

Harri snort laughed.

"What? They're new!" Tyrone said.

"It's OK," Jase said. "We're all scared. But if we do it together, we can be quick! And at least we know he's not a ghost," Jase said with forced cheeriness. "Ghosts don't drink tea."

Tyrone twisted his face, chewing on his cheek. "OK. In and out."

Jase snuck forward. When he got to below the open window he turned to see if the others were behind him. He was blinded by a beam of light.

"Head torch," Harri said, like an explanation was needed. "It's my dad's."

Jase pulled his torch out too. It gave out a weak blue light. The batteries needed changing.

Kinga pulled her torch out, while Tyrone turned on his phone's flashlight.

Suddenly, stars and planets danced around the mouldy walls of the caravan. They were coming from Kinga's bright pink projector torch.

They all gave her a LOOK.

"What?" Kinga said. "It's the only one I had."

"Just share mine," Jase said.

Kinga killed the light.

"Give me a bunk up," Harri said. "I can sneak in the window and open the door for the rest of you."

That was a better idea than all of them trying to get in the small window.

Jase and Tyrone linked hands and boosted Harri up.

She reached through the window and pushed her arms and head inside. Her legs waggled around outside. And then she slithered through the gap and vanished. A second later, there was an almighty crashing sound.

Jase winced along with the others. It didn't sound like Harri had had a very soft landing.

Harri's face appeared in the window as she pulled aside the curtains and gave them all a cheery thumbs up.

At least she was alive. But they'd be lucky if they hadn't woken everyone up with all that noise.

Harri disappeared again. There was the sound of more thuds and thumps as Harri made her way towards the door. She hadn't been wrong about having terrible coordination.

At last, the door opened. Hari's hair was even more wild than usual. One of her buns had come loose and the other had a fork stuck in it. But she was grinning.

"Welcome," she said, waving them inside.

Tyrone was first through the door. He clearly wanted to get this over and done with as quickly as possible.

Kinga was next. Jase closed the door behind them.

Jase traced his torch around the room. It was full of clutter. Piles of books and newspapers. Old letters and empty food cans. Whoever lived here wasn't taking very good care of themselves.

"Can't see any of the stolen stuff," Harri said, pulling open drawers and looking in the cupboards.

Jase moved to the back of the van. There was only one door, which opened on to a small bathroom. There was less mess in here, but no sign of stolen watches or gnomes. Maybe the thief kept them somewhere else? Jase shut the door quickly.

"I think I got something!" Tyrone said.

Jase returned to where Tyrone was standing by the small kitchen table. He was pointing his torch at a scrap of paper on the table.

It was a receipt. Jase picked it up to read it.

"It's for medication from a chemist in Chesterfield," he said. "Dated Saturday at five fifteen p.m."

"Oh, I saw a bag from a chemist!" Kinga said. She directed them towards a white paper bag on the kitchen table with a green cross on it. It was still sealed closed, the medicine inside untouched.

"Why would he be getting medication from Chesterfield?" Tyrone asked. "He could just get it from the chemist in town?"

"I don't know, but we do know that if he was in Chesterfield on Saturday..." Jase said.

"There was no way he would be back here in time to steal the stuff," Harri said.

Jase felt a heavy guilt swirling in his stomach. He had been so sure that the thief was the man who lived here. But he'd been wrong.

"I feel bad for him," Kinga said, holding up one

of the cans. "Looks like the only thing he eats is spaghetti hoops."

She was right. There was no other food in the place besides tinned spaghetti.

"OK, we've had our look," Tyrone said. "It's not him. Let's get out of here."

Jase agreed. The sooner he could get out of the oppressive heat of the caravan, the better he would feel.

He turned to go when he heard the twisting of the door handle.

There was nowhere to hide. They were caught.

CHAPTER NINETEEN

The moment between hearing the twisting of the door handle and the door opening seemed to last for ever. They all froze. They looked to each other for answers. No one had any.

At last, Tyrone said, "Hide!"

Harri threw herself behind the armchair. Kinga hid behind the tatty curtains. Tyrone crawled under the small kitchen table. Which left Jase. He didn't know where to hide. He looked around for somewhere. Anywhere. The door was opening. The bogeyman was getting closer. Jase dived to the floor and rolled under the bed.

He heard feet pounding on the floor. No normal

human could make footsteps that loud. The bogeyman had to be a giant. He heard the door slam. Louder even than the pounding of his heart in his chest. He held his breath so the sound of his panicked wheezing wouldn't give him away. The feet moved closer. Any second now, he would be dragged out and the bogeyman would … what? Rip his arms off and cook him up as a nice change from spaghetti hoops?

"It's OK," a gentle voice said. "You can all come out."

Nothing happened.

The man spoke again. "I can see you behind the curtains. And you, behind the chair and under the table. And … those shoes poking out from under my bed."

There was nothing for it. Jase rolled back out.

The others emerged from their hiding places.

Up close, the man looked less like an ogre and more like a normal man who could do with a shave. He had light brown eyes that twinkled amid the mess of shaggy hair and beard. He was wearing a white polo shirt and khaki shorts and trainers. All of which had seen better days.

"Well then," the man said, not unkindly. "What's going on here?"

Harri stepped forward. She took a deep breath. "We're investigating who has been stealing things from the caravan site because Mr Collins thought it was me but it's not me I haven't been stealing anything but someone has and we needed to find out who before Mr Collins kicked us off and banned us for life so we made it our summer mission besides I wanted to get my Switch back and we interviewed everyone and got a timeline and Jase found his birthday coin in the pusher which means the thief had been at the Coast and we hacked the CCTV which was easier than it should have been and I really should talk to Mr Collins about his cyber security and we saw that two people had used the pusher and one of them was my brother Oliver who is a massive loser but he couldn't have stolen Mr Graves' ugly gnome the one doing the moony as he wasn't here and the other person had a pink fluffy rabbit and we followed the rabbit to the pub but the bouncer lady wouldn't let us in so Kinga and Jase did the two kids

201

under a trench coat thing and got in and made a film and we saw the pink rabbit and then we saw you and we snuck in here to see if you were the thief but now we see it can't be you and please don't kill us."

The words flew out of Harri like ping-pong balls tumbling down a staircase. Each word rushing out after each other.

"I didn't catch most of that," the man said, his words slow and deliberate. "Anyone want to try again?"

Tyrone cleared his throat. "Hello, sir. My name is Tyrone. And these are my friends, Kinga, Jase, and that's Harri. We call ourselves the Castle Rock Crew, which isn't important. But what is important is that we care very much about this caravan site. And when we heard things were going missing, well, we thought it was our duty to help."

"Your duty?" the man said, the faintest smile twitching at the corner of his mouth.

"Indeed. And after a thorough investigation, the clues led us to you. And so, yes, we thought you were the thief, and we did sneak in, and we're so incredibly sorry to have bothered you and we will be happy to carry out any chores for you to apologize. And please don't tell our parents."

"Thief, hey?"

They all nodded.

"Well," he said, scratching his beard. "What do we do?" He looked more confused than angry. He smiled, as if an idea had occurred to him. Jase hoped it didn't involve eating any of them. "How about we start with a cup of tea?"

The relief Jase felt was better than getting off the roller coaster.

The man walked over to the kettle. Kinga and Harri shuffled out of his way. Jase noticed he was a bit wobbly on his feet and had to steady himself using the countertop. He picked the kettle up and then seemed to forget what he was going to do with it. Jase had a familiar feeling.

"Let me," he said, taking the kettle off the man. "You sit down."

The man smiled and did as Jase instructed, moving

over to the bed. The springs made a loud *spur-rring* sound as he sat down.

Jase dug around the tiny kitchen for mugs and tea bags. He only found one tea bag in a glass jar, which he used to make the man a cup of tea. For the others he poured cold water into mugs and handed them out.

Jase noticed the man's hands shook a little as he took his mug.

He slurped his tea. "That is a good cuppa. My … my name is Bob." Each word he spoke was precise, almost as if he had to fight to sound out each one. "I … I didn't catch all of your names."

The crew re-introduced themselves.

"Tell me again … about your thief. But do an old man a favour. Go slowly."

Jase didn't think Bob looked *that* old. He was probably in his early fifties. But he spoke and moved like a much older man.

Between them all, they filled Bob in. He nodded in the right places and made the right noises.

They showed him the video from the pub and he nodded.

"I … I found that pink rabbit. Thought Callie in the pub would like … like it for her littl'un."

That was one mystery solved. But they were still no closer to finding their thief.

"I'm sorry, though. I don't know … anything about any thefts. I used to know everything that went on around Castle Rock," Bob said with a sigh. "I … I was the postie here for over thirty years. A person's post, you see … it tells you a lot about them. You know when it's their birthday. When their loved ones pass. You know when they get new jobs. When … when they can't pay their bills." Speaking looked like it was an effort for Bob. He spoke slowly and carefully and paused to take a breath after each sentence. And yet the crew hung on his every word. "We deliver the good news. And we deliver the bad. We're there for the ups … the ups and downs of life, six days a week. Rain or shine. We know everyone's names. And yet, most people don't bother to ask ours."

He was right, Jase thought. The same postie came every day to their flat at home and he didn't know her name. He made a promise to ask her the next time he saw her.

"It's an honour to be a postie. Greatest job in the world."

"Then why, if you don't mind me asking," Kinga said, "did you stop?"

"They made me take early retirement. My health… The doctors said I had a mini stroke. I've struggled since then. I get sleepy during the day and I'm up all night. And my memory… I can remember things from twenty years ago sharp as anything. But I'll be honest, kids, most of what you've told me tonight, I probably won't remember tomorrow."

Jase recognized all the symptoms Bob was describing.

"My nana is the same," he said. "She has dementia. I help look after her, but it's not always easy."

Kinga and Harri looked at Jase in surprise.

"Ah," said Bob. "Well then."

"Are you getting help?" Jase asked. He looked around the messy camper and thought he already knew the answer.

"I was sent to the Chesterfield Royal Hospital for an assessment on Friday. They sent me away with all these leaflets and prescriptions. I stayed with my old postie mate, Dave, and he got all the pills for me."

That explained the receipt from Saturday.

"But I didn't tell him what they were for. I didn't want to worry him."

Jase looked over at the unopened chemist bag. It seemed that Bob wasn't following the doctors' advice.

No one said anything for a while. They sipped from their mugs.

"There is one thing I remember. And it might just help with your investigation," Bob said.

"What?" Harri said.

"Let me see your video again. Of the pub."

They played Bob the video again. He tapped on the screen as it panned across the old lady at the bar.

"That woman there. She isn't who she seems."

"What?" Tyrone said, surprised. "Old Beryl?"

"She used to live in town. In a small flat over a chippy." He closed his eyes and plucked the address from his memory. "6B High St, Skegness PE25 3NY." He tapped the side of his head. "Never forget my old route." As he started to talk about the past, the words came easier. Jase had seen this with his nana too. It was as if the past was easier for them to connect to than the present. "One day, about ten years ago, I delivered a postcard to Beryl. The card was addressed to her flat, but to a different name. I thought it must be a mistake, but when I handed it over to her... She looked like she'd seen a ghost. She started acting all squirrelly. Went on and on about

208

how that name wasn't hers. No way." He took a long drink of his tea before continuing. "People are always getting addresses wrong, so I didn't think anything of it. Not till she started up like that. And I thought to myself, 'the lady doth protest too much'. And so, well, I wouldn't have usually done this, but I glanced at what was written on the postcard."

"What was it?" Harri said, breathless with anticipation.

"'Run.'"

"What?" Tyrone said.

"It said, 'They're on to you. Run.'"

They all looked at each other.

"Who was on to her?" Kinga said.

"Run from who?" Tyrone said.

Bob shook his head. "I don't know that. But I do know she moved out of that flat and moved here to Castle Rock. She never recognized me, but I knew her." He tapped his head again.

"Can you remember the name?" Jase asked. "The name on the postcard?"

Bob smiled. "I might struggle to remember what happened yesterday, but I remember that. It was the kind of name you don't hear around these parts. Beryl's name, what I think is her real name, is Catherine Carter–Calthorpe."

They all leaned back and let out a collective sigh. This mystery was getting deeper by the second.

"Catherine Carter–Calthorpe," Kinga said, taking out her phone again. "Can't be many of them around."

She typed away and a moment later gasped. "No!"

"What?" Tyrone asked.

"She never!"

"What?" Harri asked.

"I can't believe it!"

"WHAT?" Jase, Tyrone and Harri all shouted at once.

Kinga turned her phone so the others could see it. The browser was open on an old newspaper article from the 1960s.

They all leaned closer to read.

Five minutes later, they all sat back and looked at each other, stunned.

Jase scratched his head in disbelief. "Looks like we found our thief."

DARING JEWELLERY THIEF TARGETS SOCIALITE MASKED BALL

Rich and famous were stunned after becoming targets of thefts during masked ball. Police looking for woman in connection with thefts.

The London Examiner, March 5, 1961

A thief masquerading as a guest at a recent ball made off with jewellery worth over half a million pounds.

The jewellery was taken from the hotel rooms of guests while the masked ball took place at the exclusive Rochester Hotel in London on Thursday night. Guests also had wallets and watches stolen during the ball, it was reported.

Miss Jenkins, 24, daughter of the multi-millionaire banker Charles Jenkins, was a guest at the ball. She returned to her hotel room to discover a pair of diamond earrings and a diamond necklace had disappeared from her nightstand.

While Mr Thompson-Thompson, 32, renowned socialite, found his Porsche had been stolen after his keys had been taken from his tuxedo pocket while on the dance floor. Police believe the Porsche may have been used as the getaway vehicle.

The police were called to the hotel on Friday morning and have interviewed everyone staying at the hotel.

"We are looking to speak to a Miss Catherine Carter-Calthorpe in connection with the thefts," said a spokesperson for the police. "And we would also like to speak to her cousin, Jack Carter."

Catherine "The Cat" Carter-Calthorpe, 21, an ex-Olympic gymnast, was seen at the ball, though organizers say her name had not been on the invite list. A woman matching her description was reportedly last seen walking out the kitchen exit, wearing a diamond necklace and earrings. Her whereabouts are unknown at this time.

Carter-Calthorpe had been arrested six months ago along with her cousin on suspicion of jewellery theft from a hotel in Bath. Both were released without charge.

If anyone has any information, they should contact Scotland Yard.

CHAPTER TWENTY

It was Wednesday morning. Four days since the thief had struck. Three days since they'd started their investigation. And, at last, Jase was sure they were on the right trail.

The crew met at Beryl's caravan and began playing a game of basketball on the grass nearby. But it was only pretend. They were there to spy on her.

The area around her caravan was beautifully maintained, with flowers of all types hanging from baskets all around. The metal walls had been painted recently and there was a single rocking chair outside. It had a cushion with a picture of a cat on the front.

"Look, a cat!" Harri said, fumbling her catch as

Tyrone threw her the ball.

"That proves nothing. All old ladies like cats," Tyrone said.

"Didn't you say you'd heard her on the phone speaking in a posh voice?" Jase asked, remembering what Harri had told him

"Yes! I did. Super posh! It's her, I know it!"

Beryl AKA Catherine The Cat *had* to be their upper-class thief. And they were going to catch her. This was what being a detective was all about. Using your brain and your bravery to catch bad people. And Jase was loving every second of it.

They could hear Beryl inside the caravan, humming along to music playing on the radio. She was badly out of tune, but she certainly didn't seem like a daring jewellery thief. But what Jase had learned from speaking to Bob last night was that appearances can be deceptive. He'd be sure to remember that when he became a detective.

He'd spoken to his auntie and nana about Bob and told them about how he had dementia too. Nicki said she would drop by to check on him and bring him some shopping. So at least some good had come from breaking into his camper van.

Jase just hoped their next break-in would be more useful for the investigation.

"What's our plan?" Jase asked, throwing the basketball to Tyrone, while still looking at Beryl's caravan.

"The windows are too small," Tyrone said. "Even if we could get one open we couldn't get through." He threw the basketball to Harri.

She fumbled her catch and dropped it. "How about we *mistakenly* smash her window with the basketball?" Harri asked, picking the ball up. She threw it to Jase.

What would Nana do? he wondered. Knock on the door, flash her badge and demand to have a look around inside. Jase couldn't wait till he was a proper police detective and then he wouldn't have to do so much sneaking around.

"That would draw too much attention. We can't make a scene until we have hard evidence she's behind the thefts," Jase said.

Tyrone threw the ball to Kinga. She caught it and instead of throwing it back, she threw it from hand to hand, staring at the caravan. "There," she said, dropping the ball and pointing. "That's how we get in."

Jase followed her finger. "The skylight?"

On top of the caravan was a domed window. It was open just a crack.

"I reckon I could squeeze through there," Kinga said.

Kinga was the smallest of the group and the only one who stood a chance of squeezing through such a small gap.

"I'm pretty sure she'd hear you stomping around on her roof," Tyrone said.

"We wait till she goes out then," Kinga said.

"Which could be all day!" Harri groaned. Jase was learning that she hated waiting for things.

But it wasn't long before the music from the radio went dead, and they saw Beryl pulling her coat on. There was the sound of bolts being unlocked inside and then Beryl opened her front door.

"All right, dustbin lids," she said.

The crew mumbled a few wary hellos. They didn't want to be too friendly to a genuine thief!

"You be careful with that ball, you hear. If one of my dahlias is so much as bruised when I get back, I'll box your ears." She shook a playful fist in the direction of Harri, who was holding the ball. Harri dropped it immediately.

Beryl sniffed and shuffled off, handbag hooked over one arm.

They waited until she turned the corner and…

"Come on," Jase said.

They didn't know how long she would be at the shops. They had maybe ten minutes, fifteen if they were lucky.

"OK, Kinga, you have a look around and we'll wait out here," Jase said. "But be quick!"

"I'll keep watch over there," Harri said, grabbing her skateboard. "If I see her coming back, I'll make the sound of a macaw."

"Won't that be a bit of a giveaway?" Tyrone asked. "You don't see flocks of macaws in Skeggy."

"An owl?" Harri said.

"Owls come out at night," Kinga said.

"Blimey! I didn't know you were such bird experts!" Harri said, exasperated. "Look, if you hear me squawk, get out of there fast."

They agreed this was a good plan. Harri jumped on her skateboard and zoomed around the corner to keep watch while Tyrone and Jase gave Kinga a leg up. She pulled herself up on to the roof of the caravan and, crawling on her belly, made her way over to the skylight.

Jase moved to the window to watch as Kinga lowered herself down on to the kitchen sideboard and from there dropped on to the floor. She made an "OK" symbol with her thumb and fingers.

Jase pressed his nose against the window, trying to have a good look inside. He had been expecting doilies and more pictures of cats. But Beryl's caravan was more like an antique shop – one of the stylish kinds. Bookshelves lined the walls. Leather-bound hardbacks nestled next to brass curios and antique typewriters.

Kinga started rifling through the bookshelves, pulling books out and flicking through the pages.

"Look in any boxes," Jase shouted through the window.

Kinga nodded and started opening anything that could be hiding jewels. Jase checked his watch. It had been five minutes already and Kinga hadn't found anything. Maybe if he joined her in the search?

He was walking up to the front door when suddenly a high-pitched shriek came from the corner. Harri's signal. Beryl was on her way back.

Jase banged on the door. "Get out!"

"One second," Kinga replied. "I think I've found something." She was holding what looked to be a photo album.

Tyrone yanked on Jase's sleeve and pulled him away from the caravan just as Beryl turned the corner. Kinga was still inside. They could see her panicked face in the window. Jase had to buy her enough time to get out. But how?

As Beryl stomped towards them, Jase jumped in front of her.

He opened and closed his mouth, trying to think of something to say. Beryl narrowed her eyes and looked from him to the door of her caravan.

"What are you up to, lad?"

"I wanted to ask you about the thefts on Saturday night!" Jase said, the words tumbling out before he had a chance to think them through.

"Did you now? Bit nosy, ain't you? Guess you take after your grandma."

"You know my nana?" Nana Rose hadn't mentioned

knowing Beryl. But with her memory being what it was that didn't count for much.

Beryl smiled. "Oh, Rose and I go way back." She sniffed again. "Well, go on then. Ask your questions. I haven't got all day."

He couldn't just come out and accuse her, but he needed to keep her talking. Tyrone moved behind him, trying to position his body between Beryl and the door to block her view.

"Where were you on Saturday night?" Jase took his notebook out with trembling hands.

"I was at the bookies watching the boxing, weren't I? I had a bet on Jax Divine. He won me fifty quid!"

"And did you see anyone strange on the site?"

Beryl made to sidestep him, but Jase moved with her, staying in front. He had no idea what was happening behind him. He just hoped that Kinga had got out.

"Everyone who comes to this place is a little bit strange, if you ask me," she said, giving Jase a pointed look.

"You didn't have anything stolen?" Jase said.

"Steal from me?" Beryl laughed, a cold, serious laugh. "No one would dare."

Jase noticed Beryl squeeze her handbag tight to her side. There was something in there she didn't want anyone seeing.

Beryl went to move to the right, but when Jase tried to follow her, she ducked to the left, spinning like a footballer getting past a defender. She was surprisingly light on her feet.

There was nothing between her and the door now. Jase looked around to see if Kinga had made it out. He caught Tyrone's eye. Tyrone gave the tiniest shake of his head. Kinga was still inside.

Beryl stomped up the steps to the caravan and stopped as she reached into her handbag, looking back over her shoulder at the boys. Jase and Tyrone pretended to be interested in something in the distance.

Out of the corner of his eye, Jase saw her pull out her key and put it in the lock. He prayed Kinga had found somewhere to hide.

Instead of opening the door, Beryl twisted the key

in the lock and then put the key back in her pocket.

"Forgot to lock up, didn't I?" she said, shuffling away. She winked at Jase as she passed.

There was something about that wink that sent a shiver down his spine. As if she knew that he knew and was toying with him. He almost shouted out there and then, accusing her of being the thief. But he needed evidence.

"Phew!" said Tyrone, clutching his chest. "I thought we were done for."

They ran back to the caravan and peered through the window. They couldn't see Kinga anywhere; she must be hiding. Jase rapped on the window with his knuckle. After a moment, Kinga's head appeared from behind the settee. She waved the photo album triumphantly above her head.

"I got her!"

"There's no time for that! Get out!" Tyrone shouted.

Kinga ran towards the door. There was the sound of her rattling the doorknob. Again and again.

She ran back to the window. "It's locked!"

Had Beryl known all along that Kinga was in there? Had she locked the door on purpose? What were they going to do?

Harri came zooming back towards them on her skateboard. "Beryl's not going to the shops. She's leaving the site!"

Jase looked from Harri back to Kinga.

"You have to go after her," Kinga shouted. "She's the thief!"

"How do you know?" Tyrone asked.

Kinga opened up the photo album and pressed it against the window. Instead of photos, there were newspaper clippings.

DARING CAT BURGLAR STILL AT LARGE

POLICE BAFFLED BY JEWELLERY THEFTS

**HAS GOLD MEDALLIST GYMNAST
SET HER SIGHTS ON DIAMONDS?**

"It *is* her!" Jase said, punching the air. They had the evidence they needed. They'd caught their thief.

"Amazing," Tyrone said. "But what good is it if you're trapped?"

"Don't worry about me. I'll find a way out," Kinga said.

"We can't just leave you locked in there," Jase said. And yet, he knew they couldn't let Beryl get away.

His nana had said that being a good detective was all about trusting your gut. At last, he knew what she meant. And his gut was screaming at him: Beryl was up to something.

"Don't just stand there," Kinga said. "Follow that old lady!"

CHAPTER TWENTY-ONE

There was an art to shadowing, Nana Rose had told Jase. And it wasn't anything like you saw in the movies.

"If coppers went creeping around like that, they'd be spotted in a snap. None of that hiding behind newspapers or lurking in doorways nonsense. You just gotta act normal."

As the crew started to follow Beryl off the site, Tyrone and Harri were acting anything but normal. They ducked from tree to tree, diving to the ground every time it looked like Beryl might glance over her shoulder. They might as well have been carrying a big sign that said "we're following you!"

Beryl stopped for a moment to readjust her red

handbag. Harri dived behind a dustbin and managed to knock it over. Luckily, Beryl didn't hear the *CRASH* and kept on walking.

Jase helped Harri back to her feet and picked a piece of lettuce off her shoulder. "Look, just act natural! She's on her way to the seafront and so are we. Simple. You keep jumping around and she's sure to notice something's up."

"Shouldn't we have a disguise?" Tyrone asked. "I could go get my uncle's trench coat again?"

The idea of hiding under the stinking coat didn't appeal to Jase. "Let's just keep walking and stay far enough behind her that she doesn't hear us, OK?"

After that, Harri and Tyrone followed Jase's lead, walking as casually as possible. They tailed her off the site and towards the seafront, always trying to keep more than ten metres back. But when they reached the seafront, Beryl slipped into the flow of the crowd of tourists, and they had to close the gap. For a heart-thudding moment, Jase thought they'd lost her, but then he spotted her standing at a stall selling sunglasses, just a few metres ahead. If they stopped walking now, it would look suspicious.

"Follow me," he whispered to the other two.

Instead of stopping behind Beryl, Jase used one of the tricks his nana had told him. He walked straight past Beryl, chatting away with Tyrone and Harri, and kept going as if they hadn't even noticed her. He took the first left they came to and only then did he stop, dragging the other two in behind him. They pressed themselves against the wall, while Jase risked peeking back at Beryl.

Beryl was still at the stall, trying to choose between two pairs of glasses: one red and one pink. She kept trying each pair on. He couldn't be sure, but he thought she might be looking behind her in the mirror of the stand. That was a neat trick he wish he'd thought of.

At last, she put both pairs down, looked over her shoulder, and scuttled back in the direction they'd come from. So, she *was* up to something!

"Come on," Jase said, pulling Tyrone after him.

"You're so good at this," Harri said as they wove between the holidaymakers and stallholders.

"Nana and I spent an afternoon practising shadowing by following my mum. We tailed her all the way from the flat to the supermarket, waited for her outside as she shopped for groceries, then followed her to the baker's where she grabbed a sausage roll."

"Did she spot you?"

"Only when we hid in a bush. We were giggling so much we made the leaves shake."

"Your nana is amazing," Tyrone said.

Jase smiled. He was right. He only wished she could be here with him. She'd love this as much as he did.

They followed Beryl away from the crowds of the seafront and along the coast, always staying far enough behind her to not be spotted, but close enough not to lose her.

Just as the beachfront was coming to an end, she turned away from the coast and wove her way up through the grass-covered dunes.

"Where is she going? There's nothing this way for miles!" Tyrone said.

"Maybe she's buried the stolen goods out here

somewhere?" Jase said.

They clambered up the dunes, spotting a flash of red handbag in the distance. She seemed to be heading towards a low concrete building that was half-buried in the sand.

They crept as close as they dared and then knelt down behind a bush of beachgrass.

"Looks like an abandoned World War Two bunker," Tyrone whispered. "We did a project on them for school."

"The perfect place to stash stolen goods," Harri replied. "I bet she has diamonds and all sorts hidden in there."

They watched as Beryl looked over both shoulders and then vanished inside the bunker.

"What now?" Tyrone said, keeping his voice low.

"If we can get a photo of her with the stolen things, we'll have the evidence we need to go to the police," Jase said.

"I wish Kinga was here," Harri said. "Her phone has the best camera."

"This will have to do," Jase said, pulling his phone out.

He put his finger to his lips and walked forward. It was hard going. The midday sun beat down on them, and away from the cool sea breeze the air was hot and sticky. Jase's trainers kept sinking into the sand. There was more sand in there than foot.

Tyrone was having the same problem. "Why didn't I bring my mud savers?" he muttered, slightly out of breath. "My Jordans are getting scuffed."

At last, they reached the bunker. It was about four metres by four metres and looked like it might go down deeper into the ground. It had been made from thick concrete blocks and built to withstand bombs. But eighty years of wind and rain had taken their toll, and now the building looked like it might fall over with a push. Grass grew on the roof and the whole structure looked like it was sinking into the sand.

The door was open a crack and a padlock hung loose on a lock. Beryl must have unlocked it to get in. Jase thought he could hear movement from deep inside. He and Tyrone put their hands against the door and *pushed*.

It was hotter in there than outside. Heavy and thick, like walking into the bathroom after Jase's mum had one of her long soaks. He tugged at the neck of his T-shirt, trying to let some air get to his skin. No air moved in there.

The only light came from one small window high in the wall. The place was a mess, with broken crates piled in the corner and faded drink cans scattered on the floor. It smelled strongly of rotting fish.

"Down there," Jase mouthed, pointing towards a staircase that led deeper down into the bunker.

They picked their way through the debris, stepping over puddles of cold, black water, and headed towards the stairs.

Tyrone took one step ahead. "Are we sure about—"

There was a sickening *CRACK*. Tyrone just had time to gasp before he fell through the floor, like a magician vanishing through a trapdoor.

Jase threw himself forward and scrambled over to the hole. He forced himself to look down. *Please be OK.*

Please be OK, he thought.

Tyrone was dangling in the hole, clutching a bent pipe. The darkness beneath him seemed to stretch out forever.

"I got you." Jase grabbed Tyrone's wrist with both his hands. "I got you!"

But Jase's hands were slippery. It was only a matter of time before Tyrone fell through his grip.

Tyrone flailed his legs, as if trying to find footing on

the air. One of his beloved trainers fell off, spiralling down into the darkness like a sycamore seed.

"Grab my legs!" Jase shouted at Harri.

Harri grabbed Jase's legs and slowly, centimetre by centimetre, the two of them pulled Tyrone back out of the hole to safety.

The three of them lay panting on the floor.

"That was too close," Jase said.

He peered back into the hole. It was so deep he couldn't see the bottom. It must have been a mine shaft or something. He could hear the sounds of water splashing deep, deep below.

"I lost my shoe," Tyrone said miserably. "It was my second favourite pair."

"At least that's the only thing you lost," Harri said. "You could have died."

"She's right," Jase said. "This is too dangerous." His obsession with catching the thief had almost got one of his friends killed. He wasn't a real police detective. What had he been thinking? "Let's get out of here."

He crawled to his knees and was helping Tyrone

stand when they heard a small cough.

"All right, dustbin lids?"

They looked up to see Beryl standing between them and the only way out.

She was holding a gun.

CHAPTER TWENTY-TWO

The gun was tiny! No bigger than her palm. But it was still a gun, and it was still pointed at them.

She gestured for them to step away from the hole. "What 'ave we here then?" she said.

There was no point in pretending any more. "We know you're a thief, Beryl," Jase snapped. "Or should I say Catherine Carter-Calthorpe?"

"Kinga found the newspaper clippings," Tyrone said, taking a small step in front of Jase and Harri. "It's all over for you!"

Beryl/Catherine lowered her pistol a fraction. A smile inched across her mouth.

"Well now. It seems you have discovered my secret,"

she said, all trace of the thick cockney accent gone. She spoke in a cut-crystal posh accent, every syllable pronounced, every T sharp. "So, what do you plan on doing about it?"

Catherine sat down on an upturned crate, her shoulders drawn back and crossed one leg over the other, brushing her skirt down over her legs. She placed her gun neatly on her lap.

"If you give back everything you took, maybe we won't have to do anything," Jase said.

"Oh, the diamonds are long gone, I'm afraid."

"We don't mean the diamonds," Harri said. "We mean my Switch and Kinga's camera and ... and Mr Graves' gnome."

In the distance, Jase thought he heard a familiar sound. The sound of barking. But maybe it was just the cawing of a crow.

"A garden gnome?" Catherine burst out laughing. "A garden gnome! What would I be doing with a garden gnome? Wait..." Catherine looked at them in confusion, her brow wrinkled. "You don't think ...

I have been stealing from Castle Rock?"

"Well, you are a cat burglar!" Jase said.

Catherine laughed. It was clear and high, nothing like the husky laugh she had been putting on as Beryl. "I *was* a cat burglar, you mean. One of the best, if I say so myself. After my career as a gymnast ended, I suppose you could say I redirected my skills to break-ins. But I hung up my leather gloves a long time ago. Besides, I only ever stole from the naughty rich folk. People who deserved it."

"What about Mrs McGinty's diamond earrings?" Harri said. "They were stolen right from her bedside table while she slept."

"Oh, those earrings are as fake as a conman's smile. They may sparkle, but they're just glass. Besides, I truly was at the bookmaker's in town watching the boxing. You can ask any of the regulars."

"If you're not guilty, why lead us all the way out here?" Jase asked.

"Well, you seemed to be having such a good time shadowing me, I thought I'd make it interesting for you."

She stood up and raised the gun at them again. "Besides, this is the perfect spot to lock you all up. The only way out is through the door, which is much sturdier than it looks. You could take your chances down the mineshaft, but I wouldn't risk it. Don't worry. I'm sure they'll find you eventually, in a day. Or three."

Panic clutched at Jase's chest. Was she really going to lock them up in here? Then, he heard it again. Clearer this time. Definitely barking.

Catherine didn't hear anything. She took a few steps towards the door. "Well, I guess I'll be on my way."

Just as Catherine reached out to open the door, it flew open with an almighty thwack, knocking her off her feet and sending the gun skidding across the floor.

There, standing with her fists pressed into her hips, Sherlock at her side barking for all he was worth, was...

"Kinga!" Jase, Harri and Tyrone said at once.

Catherine scrabbled on the floor for the gun, but Harri was too fast.

She snatched it up and pointed it at the woman. "Don't move!"

Catherine raised her hands in defeat.

"Are you all OK?" Kinga asked. Her usually neat hair looked dishevelled and there was a tear in the knee of her jeans that Jase didn't remember seeing earlier. "What happened to your trainer?"

"It fell down there," Tyrone said, pointing at the hole in the floor.

"And he nearly fell down with it!" Harri said.

"Oh my god, are you sure you're OK?"

"We're fine," Tyrone said. "Are *you* OK?"

She nodded.

"How did you find us?" Jase asked.

"I climbed back out through the skylight, which wasn't easy, let me tell you. And then I went and asked your aunt and nana if I could borrow Sherlock. He followed your scent and led me all the way here. And just in time."

Sherlock spun around twice and barked, happy to have done his job.

"Clever boy!" Jase said, scratching Sherlock on the head. His tail thudded against the floor.

"Well, isn't that nice," Catherine said, slowly getting to her feet. She brushed dirt off the back of her skirt and readjusted the bow of her silk shirt. "But I think you should put that gun down before you hurt yourself."

"Don't take one more step!" Harri said.

"Or what? You'll shoot? You've never shot a gun in your life!"

Harri lowered the gun just a fraction. A wicked smile spread over her face. Jase had seen Harri shooting ducks on the seafront games and killing zombies in the arcades. She was an amazing shot. She took aim at a spot on the ground just in front of Catherine's shoes, closed one eye and pulled the trigger.

Jase closed his eyes, waiting for the deafening bang. There was a click. A small blue flame flickered from the end of the gun. It wasn't a gun after all. It was a cigarette lighter.

Harri looked at the gun in shock.

"Filthy habit," Catherine said, taking the lighter out of Harri's shaking hand. She held it up to her lips and blew out the flame. "I gave up smoking years ago, but this lighter was given to me by the Duke of Buckinghamshire, so I couldn't throw it away." She slipped the lighter back into her handbag.

Jase thought he saw the glint of something sparkling inside. But it could have just been a beam of light reflecting off the metal handle of the lighter.

Harri's nostrils were flaring. She hated losing.

"Oh, don't look at me like that," Catherine said. "I wasn't really going to lock you up in here. I was going to leave the door unbolted."

"So what are you going to do now?" Kinga asked. "We have evidence you're a wanted criminal."

Catherine waved Kinga's threat away. "Oh, please, those crimes were decades ago. And what proof do you really have?"

She was right, Jase thought. The newspaper clippings weren't hard evidence. Who would believe that this old lady was a criminal mastermind?

The others looked as disappointed as he did. Tyrone kicked at a stone with his socked foot. Harri's bottom lip was so baggy she could have carried her shopping in it.

"So, how about we make a trade?" Catherine said.

"What kind of trade?" Jase asked. Was she going to try to bribe her way out of this with some of her stolen diamonds? His nana had told him about corrupt police and how easily they could be bought.

"I will give you some information about how to catch your bandit, and you'll let me go."

Jase looked to the others. They all seemed to be thinking the same thing. They wanted to catch the Castle Rock thief more than anything. And Catherine's crimes had been a long time ago.

"Go on then," Jase said. "But this had better be good."

Catherine chuckled. "You really do take after your nana. Well, here is my insider tip." She tapped the side of her nose. "You said that Mabel's earrings were stolen from her bedside table while she slept?"

They all nodded.

"In a creaky old caravan where every movement can be heard? Impossible. Even a legendary cat burglar like myself wouldn't be able to pull off that heist!"

It wasn't quite the information Jase had been hoping

for. He'd been hoping Catherine would have outright told them who the thief was. But they'd made a deal.

Catherine gave them a curt nod and turned to go. She stepped over the broken door and paused, looking back. "Can I ask: how did you find me?"

"Bob," Jase said. "The postman. He delivered you a postcard which had your real name on it."

Catherine nodded. "My cousin Jack. I gave him my address in case of emergencies and the fool used my real name to notify me that the police were on to me. Shame, I liked that flat. But I couldn't bring myself to leave Skegness. I love this place." She looked out through the doorway, a soft smile on her face. "Well, good luck, my young detectives. And one more thing..." Her graceful posture suddenly vanished as she bent over. "One word to the coppers and I'll do ya, you hear me?"

Beryl was back.

CHAPTER TWENTY-THREE

They trudged back to the caravan site, heads hanging low. The only one who spoke was Tyrone, and that was to complain about how his sock was getting wet.

Jase felt terrible about Tyrone losing his shoe. He felt terrible about everything. He'd been so focused on catching the thief he'd put his friends in danger. Not to mention leaving Kinga trapped in a caravan. Wasn't it a police officer's job to look after people? Maybe he wasn't cut out for it after all.

"Oh my god!" Kinga said as they got to the arcades. "What's wrong with us?"

"Well, we failed," Jase said.

"We didn't find the buried treasure," Harri said.

"I lost one of my Jordans." Tyrone waggled a soggy sock in Kinga's direction.

"But don't you see? There is still a mystery to solve!" Kinga said, beaming. "And what is it that the Castle Rock Crew do?"

Tyrone smiled. "We solve mysteries!"

"Exactly! So, OK, we got it wrong. But as Sherlock Holmes would say, 'the game is still afoot!'"

Sherlock barked at the mention of his name.

A bubble of excitement rippled in Jase's belly. Kinga was right. There was still a crime to solve and a thief to bring to justice. And he knew exactly what their next step should be.

"Come on," he said, starting to run back towards the site. "We need to speak to Mrs McGinty!"

Ten minutes of running later, Jase stopped at the steps of Mrs McGinty's caravan to get his breath back. A stitch was stabbing his side. His nana had forgotten to remind him that there was another thing a police detective would need. Fitness!

"What's the plan?" Kinga asked. She was a bit red in the face and out of puff too.

Even Tyrone was looking a little flushed. He had given up trying to run in just one shoe and had taken the remaining one off, running all the way back in his socks. He was still carrying the trainer, though. He couldn't bring himself to throw it away.

"You don't think Mrs McGinty is the thief?" Harri said.

Jase shook his head. He wasn't ready to start accusing more old ladies!

"What Beryl said got me thinking," Jase said. "If we can work out how Mrs McGinty's earrings were stolen, it might bring us closer to knowing who did it!"

He knocked at the door.

They listened to the loud creaking of the caravan as Mrs McGinty crossed the floor to answer the door.

She peered down at them. "Have you found my missing earring?"

"Not yet," Jase said. "But we wondered if we could have a look around. At the scene of the crime."

Mrs McGinty sniffed. "Well, if you must. But *that* has to stay outside!"

The "that" referred to Sherlock. Jase didn't trust people who didn't like dogs, but he told Sherlock to stay anyway.

Sherlock wagged his tail and lay down by the door.

"The earrings were taken from in here," she said, leading them through the caravan to her bedroom.

The caravan squeaked and moaned with every step they took.

"This is one creaky old caravan," Tyrone said.

Jase agreed. Mrs McGinty was small and frail, and even she couldn't move without making a loud noise. How on earth had the thief managed it?

"There." Mrs McGinty pointed to a small china plate on the bedside table. One diamond earring lay there, the one that had been found outside Harri's window. "*Both* my earrings were there when I went to bed and gone when I woke up."

Jase walked closer to the bed. *Creak. Creak. Creak.* The floor really was loud.

"Are you a deep sleeper, Mrs McGinty?" Jase asked.

"Quite the opposite. Even the slightest sound wakes me up."

"Hmmm," Jase said.

He walked over to the window. There was a crystal sun catcher hanging from the latch. Jase turned it until it caught the sun's rays and sent sparkling rainbow lights around the room.

"My granddaughter gave me that," Mrs McGinty said. "It catches the early morning sun and wakes me up."

"Hmmm," Jase said again. Another clue to add to the others.

The window was the type that only opened at the top. It was open a crack, letting in cool air. "Do you sleep with this window open?"

"Well, yes, but you don't think the thief came through there, do you?"

Jase shook his head. Even Kinga couldn't squeeze through a window that tiny, so whoever stole the earrings would have had to come through the door. But that didn't make any sense, either. They'd have to be lighter than air not to make a sound walking across the floor.

Something his nana had said came back to him. *"What kind of thief would go to the effort of stealing the earrings only to be foolish enough to drop one?"*

He looked out the window and smiled. "What kind of thief doesn't make a sound?"

"Are you saying a ghost stole the earrings?" Kinga said. She grabbed hold of Tyrone's arm, as if ready to throw him in front of any ghost that might turn up.

"What have I said about ghosts?" Harri said.

"No, not a ghost. Look!" He pointed out the window.

The others gathered around to see what he was pointing at. A big oak tree stood between Mrs McGinty's and Harri's caravans. In it, hopped a pair of magpies.

"I think I might have found your thief," he said.

They walked over to the tree and looked up. The magpies had built a nest in the top branches. Something glinted in the light.

"Can someone give me a leg up?" Jase asked.

Tyrone boosted Jase up to the first branch. The

magpies squawked in disapproval at having someone in their tree and flew off to watch from a caravan roof. Jase wasn't the best at climbing trees, but he didn't have to go too high up till he could peer into the nest. There, amid ring pulls and bits of tinsel, was Mrs McGinty's missing earring. He hooked it out and clambered back down the tree.

"The magpie must have been attracted to your window by the sun catcher," Jase said, placing the earring in Mrs McGinty's hand when he'd climbed back down. "And then saw the earrings."

"Which explains why one was dropped outside my caravan," Harri said. "It must have dropped the earring flying back to the nest."

"Exactly."

"You're a genius," Kinga said, patting Jase on the shoulder.

He did feel pretty proud of himself for having worked it out.

"Well, well," Mrs McGinty said, closing her hand over her earring. She slipped it into the pocket of her cardigan. "Very clever…"

Jase smiled shyly, expecting a compliment.

"… of the magpie. They are such smart birds."

And without so much as a thank you, Mrs McGinty went back to her creaky caravan and shut the door.

CHAPTER TWENTY-FOUR

Patterns. Jase couldn't stop thinking about patterns for the rest of the day. His nana had said: when investigating you're always looking for patterns. They'd already found one thing that didn't fit the crime: Mrs McGinty's earrings. But what if there were other things that didn't fit?

Floating earrings and magpies and garden gnomes filled his dreams. Something wasn't adding up.

The next morning, Jase was the first to wake. He grabbed his phone and sent a text to the crew.

> **Jase:** We need to go back over all the evidence.

Kinga: You're starting to sound like a real detective. 🕵️‍♂️♂

Jase grinned. He was starting to feel like one too.

Jase: Coast. 10am

There was a string of thumbs up in response.

They met at the Coast and turned around the picture of the dancing couple to reveal their evidence board.

"Well, we can get rid of that!" Kinga said, pulling the picture of Mrs McGinty and her earrings off the board and throwing it over her shoulder.

Jase looked at the other pieces of the puzzle they had pinned to the board. The Switch, camera, the watch, the £20 and the garden gnome. He stood back and tried to see the bigger picture. One of these things didn't fit the pattern. He pulled the picture of the garden gnome off the board and looked again. Now the stolen items told a clear story: cash and items that could be easily sold for cash around the back of a bike shed without having to answer too many questions. All things a petty thief would take. Maybe even a kid.

"There's something not adding up about Mr Graves' story," Jase said.

"Hang on!" Tyrone said, clicking his fingers. "Remember when we saw him digging behind his caravan? Maybe he was burying the stolen things!"

Jase had forgotten that. Tyrone could be on to something. "There's one way to find out!" he said.

They made their way to Mr Graves' caravan and were glad to see there was no one in. With a quick look to check no one was watching, they snuck around behind the caravan. There was a pile of recently disturbed dirt. Jase got down on his hands and knees and started digging.

He pushed the soil aside and stopped when he got to what he had hoped to find.

Two pink buttocks stared up at them out of the dirt.

The others helped him dig more. There was a foot. And a hat. And finally, a head. The gnome, broken into pieces.

"Why did he say it was stolen?" Kinga said, picking the gnome's head up and brushing the dirt away from its rosy cheeks.

"So I could claim on the insurance."

They turned to see Mr Graves standing behind them. He let out a loud sigh. "That gnome was hand painted by a leading gnome artist. It cost me over two hundred pounds and I was cleaning it when … I dropped it."

Jase gathered up the pieces of the gnome in his arms. He looked from the coloured shards to Mr Graves' sorry expression. The man clearly loved these weird little creatures. But insurance fraud was a crime and they should report him.

Jase remembered what his nana had told him: *"Listen to your gut."*

His gut told him that Mr Graves was a very silly man but not a criminal. He dropped the pieces. They clattered to the ground, breaking up into even smaller shards. "There," he said. "Now you can say a kid on the site smashed it."

Mr Graves smiled. "Thank you."

They left Mr Graves reburying his beloved gnome.

"You know," Harri said, "for someone who wants to be a police officer, you are very good at getting around the law."

Jase shrugged. "Only for the right reasons."

"What are we going to do now?" Harri said, sounding as miserable as Mr Graves. "We have no more clues to follow."

"We could check everyone's alibis?" Kinga said.

"How?" Tyrone said, throwing his hands up. "There are over a hundred people on this site. That's too many people for us to check. Besides, we can't go around demanding everyone tell us where they were on Saturday night. We're not the actual cops."

Tyrone was right. They weren't really police detectives.

But he knew someone who was.

CHAPTER TWENTY-FIVE

"What we need to do now," Nana Rose said, a sparkle in her eye, "is set a trap."

They were back in the caravan with Jase's nana and his auntie. They'd brought their evidence board with them and talked her through everything they'd worked out, while Nicki made them all peanut butter sandwiches. They told her about the earrings and the magpie. About how the gnome theft didn't fit the pattern and what really happened to that. And about how the thief stuck to smaller items that could be sold easily.

Jase could see her come alive as they went over the case. And now, she seemed to have a plan.

"A trap!" Harri said. "Yes! We could dig a pit!"

"And how exactly are we going to dig a pit without Mr Collins having something to say about it?" Tyrone said, giving Harri a withering look.

"OK, OK," Harri said. "No pit. But how about a cage?" She grabbed a pen off the table and started drawing. "We could rig up a lever system attached to our bait, and when they pick it up, it could make a ball roll down a pipe like this and land on a pin like this, which would then release a cage and *BAM* they'd be caught." She threw the pen down and looked at her drawing proudly.

Jase twisted his head to try and make sense of it. It just looked like a lot of scribbles to him.

"Not that kind of trap," Nana said kindly. "Although that would be a lot of fun. No, I'm talking about something a little more subtle."

The crew drew in closer to listen to her.

"Have you heard of capture houses?" Nana asked.

"Is that like an escape room?" Kinga asked excitedly.

Nana laughed. "Sort of, only we hope that the

person who enters it doesn't get out, no matter how smart they are. No, a capture house is a technique the police use to catch burglars. We'd take an empty property and set it up to look like the kind of home we know matches our burglar's MO."

"What's an MO?" Harri asked.

"A modus operandi," Nana said. "A particular way of doing something. So, if we knew our burglar always broke into downstairs flats with no alarm systems, we'd set the capture house up like that. If we knew they targeted fancy houses, going in via open windows, we'd make a house look fancy and leave a window open. And, of course, we'd fill the capture house with the kinds of stuff we knew our burglar liked to take. Then we'd install cameras and just wait for our burglar to be lured in!"

"So, we find an empty caravan and fill it with the kind of stuff our thief likes?" Jase said.

"Exactly."

"And we set up a camera to watch their every move!" Kinga said.

"That's so sneaky," Harri said. "I love it!"

They were all so excited by this plan, they started jumping up and down. Sherlock joined in, barking and spinning around. He also let out a loud fart.

"I thought dogs were meant to help sniff clues out," Harri said, waving a notepad around to make the smell go away, "not stink up the place."

The only one not getting carried away by the excitement was Nicki. She was standing, gazing at the crime board, and sipping a cup of tea. "How are they getting in?" she asked.

"What?" Jase and his nana said at the same time.

"The thief? How are they getting into the caravans?"

That was a good question. Jase pulled out his notebook and read back over the interviews. "There's no mention of open windows or smashed glass," he said.

"So they picked the locks?" Harri said.

"Hmmm," Nana said. "That would take a pretty sophisticated thief, and this profile doesn't match that." She tapped the crime board.

"Maybe they had a key?" Nicki said.

The mention of a key lit a bulb in Jase's head.

"What's a skeleton key?" he said, remembering what had been itching away in his mind for days.

"A key that can open any lock," Nana said. "Why?"

"Something Mr Collins said. I think maybe he lost his."

"That's what he was talking about on the phone," Tyrone said.

"And what he was looking for on Saturday!" Kinga said. "No wonder he was so riled up."

Kinga scribbled a picture of a key with a skeleton head and pinned it on the board. They had the missing piece of the puzzle.

"Nicki," Jase said, hugging his auntie, "you're a genius."

"Well, I'm glad someone finally recognized it."

"So, that's the plan! We find an empty caravan and set it up as a capture house?" Kinga said.

"But where are we going to find an empty caravan?" Harri said. "They're all full."

"I have a genius idea for that too," Nicki said.

CHAPTER TWENTY-SIX

"Bob's camper van?" Tyrone asked, his nose scrunching up a little.

Jase understood his concern. Even during the day it was a bit creepy. Sherlock was still refusing to go near it. He sat a few yards away and growled. Nicki had led them all over here and was now grinning.

"Yeah, I'm not sure our thief will be lured in by this place. It's hardly that enticing," Harri said.

"That's why you'll need these," Nicki said, producing a bucket, sponges and cleaning spray. She handed the bucket and spray to Jase. His heart sank. The last thing he had been expecting to do on his holiday was chores!

Trust his auntie to turn a criminal investigation into a way of helping someone out. She had a heart as big as the world.

"Don't give me that face," she said, throwing the sponges in Harri and Tyrone's direction. "If you lot all work together you'll have this place sparkling in no time."

"Us lot?" Jase said. "So you're not helping then?"

"I'm taking Bob for lunch," Nicki said, knocking on the camper van door with a jaunty rat-a-tat-tat.

Bob opened it. He looked a little confused at first, but when he saw Nicki, he smiled. "It's been some time since I went on a date," he said, walking slowly down his stairs. Nicki gave him a hand with the last few steps. "Especially with someone as pretty as you."

"Oh, Bob," Nicki said, nudging him with her elbow. "You old charmer."

She led him away, leaving the crew to get to work.

"You know, volunteering looks good on school records," Kinga said with a smile. "Plus, it makes great content!" She grabbed a sponge from Tyrone and

started filming herself cleaning the camper van wall.

"Come on," Jase said to Tyrone. "Let's fill this up with water."

Nicki hadn't been completely wrong. With all four of them working together, it didn't take too long before Bob's camper van was starting to look half decent. Tyrone and Harri cleaned the outside, while Jase and Kinga tackled inside, cleaning the kitchen and throwing out all the rubbish. Kinga even picked some wildflowers and put them in a jar on the table. The biggest change was the smell. Instead of stinking of damp and old socks, the camper now smelled of bleach.

After a few sweaty hours, they stepped back and admired their handiwork.

"You know, this van looks pretty cool," Harri said.

"Yeah, almost retro," Kinga said, zooming in and out on the shining chrome surface.

"If I were a thief," Tyrone said, putting his arm around Jase, "I'd want to rob it."

"One final test," Jase said.

He whistled for Sherlock, who had been sleeping

under a bush outside. The dog opened one eye and sniffed the air. He stood up and kept sniffing all the way into the camper. He jumped up on Bob's settee and went back to sleep.

"I guess it passes the Sherlock test!" Kinga said. "Now all we need to do is work out what to use for bait."

They knew it had to be the kind of stuff their thief was interested in. Small items that could be easily sold.

Jase thought about everything he owned. The only thing he thought matched their burglar's MO was his mobile phone. He didn't want to risk losing it, but if it meant catching the thief...

"I guess we could use this?" he said, pulling the phone out of his jean pocket. "It's the only thing I have that our thief might want."

"Good one," Harri said. "But I think we're going to need more than that. If we want the trap to be as tempting as possible. The only thing I have is my laptop, but I'll need that for the surveillance." She looked to Kinga and Tyrone.

"I'll head back to my caravan," Kinga said. "See if Mum and Dad have anything we could use."

"Great!" Harri said as Kinga sped off.

"Well, my phone is cracked, and I don't have a laptop," Tyrone said with a shrug.

As one, Jase and Harri looked down at Tyrone's trainers.

"No way," Tyrone said when he saw what they were looking at. "I've already lost one pair today!"

"They're worth a lot," Jase said.

"Yeah, but these are vintage. Only a true sneaker-head would even know that they're worth anything. The thief would probably just think they're a stinky old pair of trainers."

"Then we use one of your other pairs," Harri said, dragging Tyrone by the arm away from Bob's camper van. "Maybe a pair you haven't worn yet. And don't tell me you don't have some still in their box!"

Tyrone protested all the way back to his caravan, but Harri wouldn't let up. And Sherlock nipped at his heels, as if trying to take the trainers off himself.

Harri shoved Tyrone inside his caravan and she and Jase waited for him to come back out.

It took over ten minutes. But at last, Tyrone emerged clutching a pair of bright white trainers to his chest.

"Perfect!" Harri said.

"But I've never even worn them!" He held them up to his face and breathed in the box-fresh smell.

"You'll get them back!" Harri said, trying to pull them away from him.

"What ya doing?" Femi, Tyrone's little sister, had followed Tyrone out to the deck.

"We're going to catch a thief," Harri said. "But we need these trainers from your brother to use as bait!"

"What if the thief gets away before we can get them back?" Tyrone said, tugging them back.

"We'll be watching," Jase said. "Even if they run, we'll know who they are, and we can follow them."

Tyrone still wasn't convinced.

"Come on, Tyrone. It's not like they're your only pair!" Harri said.

"But they're my second favourite pair!"

"You say that about every pair," Harri said. "Now give 'em over." She tried to grab them out of Tyrone's arms, but he dodged away like he was playing basketball.

Tyrone leaped over the decking banister and Harri gave chase. She followed him around the caravan, jumping over deckchairs and ducking under a hammock that swung between the caravan and a tree.

Jase, Sherlock and Femi watched them go round and round. Sherlock barking each time they ran past the front of the caravan. There was a loud crash as Harri knocked a flowerpot over.

"What is this racket?" Tyrone's mum said, appearing in the doorway.

"Sorry, Mrs Reynolds," Harri said, scooping up handfuls of soil and pouring them back into the flowerpot. It didn't look too badly damaged.

"Yeah, sorry, Mum."

"If you're going to murder each other, keep it down. I'm trying to read and your father is having a nap."

Tyrone and Harri both promised they would be

quiet. With a kiss of her teeth, Tyrone's mum shut the door again.

Tyrone still wasn't handing over his trainers.

"You can use this as bait!" Femi held up her toy: the sheep Kinga had won for her at Fantasy Island.

"But I thought he was your favourite," Harri said.

Femi gave the sheep a squeeze. "Catching a thief sounds *wery* important. And you said you'll get it back?"

"See!" Harri said, pointing at Femi. "And she's only five!"

Tyrone looked from his little sister to his trainers. He slumped and, turning his face away, held them out. "OK. Don't make me regret this!"

Harri snatched them out of his hands and shoved them into her rucksack.

Tyrone looked like he might be sick. Before he could change his mind, Kinga came running up to them.

It was a shock to see the usually calm Kinga in such a state. Her face was red and puffy and there was a snot bubble popping out of her nose.

"What's wrong?" Jase asked.

"Going ... home ... tomorrow ... morning!" she said between gulping sobs.

"Why?" Harri said.

"They want to avoid the weekend traffic!"

"But we haven't caught the thief yet!" Jase said.

"I know! And we are so close!" Kinga burst into a loud wail. "It's. Not. Fair!"

Since Jase had known her, Kinga seemed so confident and easy-going. Seeing her like this was a shock. He didn't know what to say.

Luckily, Tyrone did. "Kinga, just breathe. It will all be OK."

"But ... I won't have finished the mission," Kinga said, wiping her nose on the back of her sleeve. "I always finish everything!"

"Here." Harri pulled a handkerchief out of one of the many pockets of her boiler suit and handed it to Kinga. Kinga looked at it in shock. Who carried handkerchiefs around? She blew her nose on it anyway and went to hand it back to Harri.

"You're OK," Harri said. "You can keep it."

Kinga sank down on to the bottom step of the caravan and put her head on her knees. Sherlock padded down the steps and nudged her with his nose. She looked up and scratched him on the head.

"When I'm sad," Femi said, "my mummy sings me a song. Shall I sing it for you?"

Kinga forced a smile. "That's OK, Femi."

Femi started singing anyway. "Tears, tears go away. Sunshine on your face. Happy, happy, happy girl. La la la."

Jase was pretty sure Femi was making it up as she went along.

It made Kinga smile, though. "Thanks, Femi!"

"Any time," Femi said, wandering back inside, her job for the day done.

Harri sat next to Kinga on the step and wrapped her arm round her shoulder. "It will be OK," Harri said. "We'll fill you in on everything."

Jase sat on the other side of her. "It won't be the same without you, though."

Kinga smiled at them both. "It's not fair. If only we had more time!" she said, her bottom lip wobbling a little again.

"Then that's exactly what we'll get," Tyrone said. He vaulted over the banister and strode off.

"Where are you going?" Jase asked, standing up.

"To speak to Kinga's parents. Come on!" He waved them after him.

Jase and the other two looked at each other, and then they ran after Tyrone.

CHAPTER TWENTY-SEVEN

Kinga's parents were already packing when the crew stormed up to her caravan. There was a half-deflated crocodile sticking out of the car boot, and Kinga's mother was trying to strap a canoe to the roof rack.

"Ah," she said with a smile. "I see you've brought reinforcements. Come on in then."

They followed Kinga's mum back inside. Jase wasn't sure what Tyrone had planned, but he hoped it would be good.

Kinga's dad emerged from the bedroom dragging a large suitcase. "Kinga, love," he said, "you can't run off like that. What have we said about using your words?" He gave her a small hug.

"But it's not fair," Kinga said again. She'd stopped crying, though.

"I know, my little social justice warrior," he said. "And when you're older, you can fight to make everything fair. But for now, you have to do what we tell you. And that includes going home when we say."

"But..." She looked over at Tyrone.

He stepped forward and took on a pose like a knight facing off against a dragon. "We're here," he said, "to advocate for Kinga."

"Advocate?" Kinga's dad said, impressed.

Jase was impressed too. He didn't know what advocate meant.

"Go on then," Kinga's dad said, stepping back. "Make your case."

He sat down on the settee and Kinga's mum joined him.

Tyrone cleared his throat. "You may have heard that there have been a series of thefts taking place on Castle Rock, thefts that have made us all feel unsafe."

Kinga's parents nodded.

"We four have set ourselves a task: find whoever is behind the thefts, bring them to justice and restore Castle Rock to the place of safety and security we all know it to be."

"Very honourable," Kinga's mother said.

"We *four*," Tyrone repeated. "Your daughter included. Your daughter is a key member of the team. She is not only intelligent, but she also understands people. Understands how they think. Which is why we need her for this last and crucial phase of our investigation. We are so very close to catching the thief. And we simply can't do it without her."

Kinga flushed in pleased embarrassment.

"You want to leave tomorrow to avoid the traffic? Understandable. But I put it to you: which would be the greater crime, getting stuck in weekend traffic or leaving a thief at large? Can you, in good conscience, say that as you go to sleep in your beds at home tomorrow night, you will sleep soundly knowing that Castle Rock, our home from home, is still unsafe when you could have done something to prevent it simply by staying two more days and giving your brilliant daughter and her friends the time to solve the mystery they have promised to solve? Two more days. Two more days and I promise you we will catch the thief and you can leave knowing you helped make that happen."

There was a long, still moment as Tyrone's words echoed around the room.

Then Kinga's parents jumped to their feet and applauded.

"Bravo, Tyrone," Kinga's mum said.

"Just brilliant," her dad said.

Harri and Jase were too busy gawping at Tyrone to speak.

"Who are you and what have you done with Tyrone?" Harri said at last.

Tyrone gave a one-shouldered shrug as if what he'd just done was nothing.

"I hope I never have to come up against you in a case, Tyrone," Kinga's dad said. "My client wouldn't stand a chance!"

"Is that a yes, then?" Kinga asked.

"Against an argument like that," Kinga's dad said, "the jury is unanimous! We will stay for two more days."

The Castle Rock Crew all jumped up and down and hugged. They then pulled off the Castle Rock Handshake. For the first time since he had learned it, Jase nailed it.

"Thank you!" Tyrone said.

"And thank you, Tyrone," Kinga's dad said, shaking Tyrone's hand. "We've always known Kinga was special. But knowing she has good friends like all of you, well, that shows us who she is as a person."

"Now, about this thief, how can we help?" Kinga's mum said.

"We need some bait to trap them," Kinga said. "Something they can't resist."

"I'm putting in my phone," Jase said.

"And I'm putting in my trainers," Tyrone said, still not happy about it.

"But they'll get them back," Harri said, nudging Tyrone to try to cheer him up.

"Ah, I see." Kinga's dad looked around. "How about ... this?" He picked up an iPad and handed it over.

"Perfect!" Harri said.

"Well, I guess we can stop packing then," Kinga's mum said, kicking closed the lid of a suitcase. "Anyone fancy a movie night?"

"*Oooo,* I know just the film to watch!" her dad said excitedly. "*To Catch a Thief!*"

This was met with blank looks. None of them had heard of the film. It was very old.

"Trust me, you'll love it."

Tyrone, Jase and Harri had to check with their families that it was OK.

"Where did all that 'I put it to you' stuff come from?" Harri asked Tyrone, as they walked back to their own caravans.

"We did a debating thing in school last year. I was pretty good at it. I guess when you have a big family like mine, you get good at making your argument."

"Good?" Jase said. "You were amazing. And don't you see? You know what you should be when you grow up. A lawyer!"

"And wear a silly wig over these sharp fades?" Tyrone ran his hand over the side of his hair. "Nah. I think I'll stick with basketball player."

They all laughed.

Tyrone had been amazing. And Kinga got her extra time.

But now the clock was ticking. They had exactly forty-eight hours to catch their thief.

CHAPTER TWENTY-EIGHT

"Don't you think it looks a bit ... suspicious?" Tyone said.

They were outside Bob's camper van setting up the trap. Bob was away at a doctor's appointment Nicki had arranged for him, so they had the camper to themselves for the day. Harri had put the phone, iPad and trainers in the window. It all looked a bit too arranged.

"What do you mean?" Harri said. "Look at that stuff! How will they resist it?"

"Oh, look," Tyrone said, pretending to stroll by. "Someone just so happens to have left a bunch of cool stuff in there. How handy. I will definitely rob this place."

"Isn't that exactly what we're hoping for?" Harri said.

"Who puts *vintage* trainers in a window with an iPad and a phone! You might as well put a sign next to it saying, 'Steal me'," Tyronne shouted.

"I just might!" Harri said, shouting back.

"Calm down," Kinga said. "Harri, it's great. Tyrone and Jase, I think you're giving the thief a little too much credit. If they're smart enough to spot it's a trap, they probably don't need to be nicking stuff, OK?"

She was right. But Jase was getting nervous. What if it didn't work? What if the thief didn't take the bait? Or, even worse, what if they did and he never got his phone back? His mum would kill him.

"How about this?" Kinga said. She went inside and moved the trainers to the settee and put the phone and iPad on the kitchen table so that everything could still be seen from the window.

Tyrone admitted that it was fine.

"And you can still see the stuff on the camera?" Jase asked.

Harri opened her laptop to check. The only camera

they had to work with was an old webcam she'd found in her box of bits. It took a while for the feed to load, but the picture was clear.

Kinga gave the camera a little wave. A few seconds later, the Kinga on the screen waved back.

"This might just work," Jase said.

"It's definitely going to work," Kinga said, joining them back outside.

They gave each other a low-key version of the handshake, keeping their hands by their sides.

"What's the range on that thing?" Tyrone asked, pointing at Harri's laptop.

"Not sure. Let's see if we get a signal from the Coast."

They raced back to the games room. Harri placed her laptop on the pool table and was just checking the feed when...

"What are you lot up to?"

Jase almost squealed in shock. He'd thought they were alone, but someone had caught them.

They turned to see Oliver, Harri's brother. He wore a black hoodie, baggy jeans and boots. How was he not melting? It was a hot, sticky day and Jase and the others were all in T-shirts and shorts.

"Wouldn't you like to know?" Harri said.

Jase positioned himself in front of Harri's laptop. The last thing they needed was Oliver ruining it all.

Oliver leaned against the door frame. "Not really. Bunch of nerds like you probably just doing your homework."

"Who are you calling a nerd?" Harri said, straining to get at him while the others held her back.

Tyrone coughed and looked pointedly at her T-shirt. It had the word "Nerd" written in the style of the NASA logo.

"Yeah, well, *I'm* allowed to call myself a nerd. He isn't."

Oliver wandered around the room, dragging his finger across the surface of the game machines. He stood in front of the mural which had been painted only a year before. Jase was again struck by how different the Oliver in the picture looked. That one was dressed in bright colours and, even though you couldn't see his face, Jase imagined he was smiling. But the Oliver in front of them never smiled. And instead of colours, he wore black. They all watched him without saying a thing.

Any time he looked in their direction, they all tried to act casual. Leaning against the pool table. Looking at the ceiling as if it was fascinating. Sherlock was the only one who didn't pretend. He followed Oliver around, sniffing at him.

"Your dog is as weird as you," Oliver said, shooing the dog away.

Jase called Sherlock back to him and made him sit at their feet.

Sherlock growled. Oliver growled back.

"Look, do you want something, or what?" Kinga said at last.

"Just wanted to see what you were up to, but I realize now that I don't care. So, you have fun, nerds," Oliver said, walking back out the door. His boots dragged on the gravel as he slunk away.

"Better a nerd than whatever you are!" Harri shouted after him.

It didn't really make any sense.

"Yeah, I know," she said to the others. "I need to work on my clapbacks."

She opened her laptop again. "Damn, I'm not getting a signal," she said. "We'll need to move closer to the camper."

"My caravan is nearest," Jase said. "And I don't think my nana or auntie would mind. In fact, I think they'd like to be involved!"

Over breakfast, his nana had been excitedly asking him all about how operation "capture camper" had been going. He'd enjoyed seeing her back to her old self and was pretty sure she'd get a kick out of seeing what they were up to.

"Perfect."

Auntie Nicki and Nana Rose weren't in when Jase got home. There was a note on the table from Nicki.

"Out for lunch. Help yourself to whatever is in the cupboards but try not to eat everything. Back soon. N x"

Harri set up the laptop on the coffee table and

sat cross-legged in front of it. The others arranged themselves so they could all see the screen and then they waited.

And waited.

And waited.

By the time Auntie Nicki and Nana Rose returned, there was still no sign of the thief.

"How's it going?" Nana Rose said.

"Nothing so far," Jase explained.

"Shove over then and let me see." She nudged Kinga off the settee so she could see the laptop.

"Looks like we might be here for a while," Nicki said. "I'll get a brew on."

"It's already been HOURS!" Tyrone said with a groan.

Jase checked his watch. It was already 5.30 p.m. and nothing. How much longer could this really take?

"Well, settle in, kiddos. It could take days." Nana pushed herself up off the settee and joined Nicki at the kitchen table for a cup of tea.

"Days!" Kinga said. "But we don't have days!"

"I once ran surveillance on a capture house in Nottingham for three months before we caught our burglar."

Jase and the others looked miserable. They'd all hoped the thief would be along any minute. Maybe they needed a second plan?

What if he was able to get fingerprints from everyone? Or a lie detector test? He could interrogate everyone on the site. Jase imagined himself in a dark room, a single light bulb pointing straight in the face of his suspect, slamming his fist on a table and demanding they tell the truth.

Jase was distracted from his daydream by movement on the screen. Someone was inside the camper. And they were going for the bait! This was it: their plan had worked!

The thief wore a hoodie pulled up. Jase couldn't tell if it was a girl or a boy. They all stared at the screen. For the briefest moment the thief turned their face towards the camera.

"Oh my god," Kinga said.

"But it can't be," Jase said.

"You know them?" Nana Rose asked.

CHAPTER TWENTY-NINE

"That," Harri said, pointing at the screen, "is my loser brother."

She was right. The person caught on camera, shoving the trainers, iPad and phone into a rucksack, was Oliver.

"Well," Nana Rose said, "what are you waiting for? Get after him!"

Tyrone leaped over the table and was out the door before Jase had even stood up. The others charged out after him, hot on the heels of their thief.

"Be careful!" Nicki shouted as Sherlock jumped off the chair where he had been snoozing and followed the gang, barking all the way.

By the time they made it to Bob's camper van, Oliver was nowhere to be seen.

"What do we do now?" Tyrone said, staring through the window into the empty camper. His precious trainers were gone.

"Maybe he's gone back to your caravan?" Jase said to Harri.

Harri nodded and they turned to head back that way.

"Look!" Kinga pointed at Sherlock. The dog was running in little circles and barking, his nose barely a few centimetres from the floor.

"What is it?" Jase asked the dog.

Sherlock ran off a few metres and then came running back, barking.

"He wants us to follow him," Kinga said.

"He must have caught Oliver's scent!" Tyrone said.

"Good boy!" Jase said. His very own detective dog!

Sherlock raced off, his little paws flying on the gravel pathways. Tyrone and Harri sprinted after him while Jase and Kinga followed as quickly as they could. They weren't as fast as the others. Jase wished they'd brought the bikes as he was starting to run out of breath and a stitch was stabbing his side.

They followed Sherlock down winding paths, getting further and further away from the centre of the site, until they reached the far edges of the grounds. There were no caravans here, just the utilities to run the place. An electricity shed and big dustbins. Piles of wood and a rusty tractor. Sherlock stopped outside a run-down building. The windows were broken, and the crumbling grey walls were covered with graffiti. There was only one door. One way in and one way out.

Jase saw movement inside. Oliver was trapped.

This was it. The thrill of the chase. Jase had spent days staring at clues, piecing bits of the puzzle together, thinking until his head ached. But now he had the thief in his sights, and he wasn't going to let them get away. His heart pounded, his muscles ached, and yet he'd never felt more alive. This was what being a detective was about.

He had grown up on his nana's stories of solving crimes and chasing down criminals. And at last, he had solved a case of his own.

Just a few more steps and it would be over. Just a few more steps and…

"Wait!"

He stopped and turned slowly around. He'd come so far. He couldn't turn back now. No matter what it took, he was going to catch his thief.

Harri skidded to a halt on the gravel. She held her arms out, and the others slammed into her. "Wait," she said again. "I'm not sure I can go through with this."

Jase understood. If he had caught one of his brothers stealing, he wasn't sure he'd want to confront them either.

"Maybe you just stay outside," Kinga suggested.

Harri chewed on her lip, thinking about it. Then she swallowed hard and took a small step forward. Tyrone wasn't so patient. He charged towards the door and slammed it open with his shoulder.

There was a yelp. Then sounds of a scuffle.

Jase and the others entered the building. The floor and walls had once been tiled, but most were cracked and falling off. On one wall there was a row of shower heads. They were covered in green moss. And there was a single cubicle with the door still on. This must have once been a shower block.

Oliver and Tyrone were stood opposite each other, both holding the strap of a rucksack. They tugged it back and forth, each trying to pull it out of the other's hands. The tugs were getting increasingly aggressive, until the boys were yanking each other back and forth.

"Stop it!" Harri shouted.

Both Tyrone and Oliver stopped tugging. The rucksack fell to the ground.

Jase ran forward and snatched the rucksack away before Tyrone and Oliver could fight over it any more. He took a quick look inside. He was relieved to see his phone, the trainers and iPad were still there.

"Oliver!" Harri said. She opened and closed her mouth a few times. But no words came out. Harri, who talked more than anyone Jase had ever met, couldn't find the words.

Oliver looked like a deer caught in a headlight.

His eyes darted from the rucksack to the cubicle to the exit. But there was no escape.

Kinga moved around him and pushed open the door to the cubicle. It made a high-pitched creak as it swung on its rusty hinges. Inside was a single shelf and on it a pile of objects. There was a Switch, a camera and a watch.

All the stolen things.

"Oh, Oliver," Harri said again. This time she sounded like she was about to cry.

Oliver slumped back against the wall of the shower block and slid down to the floor, until he was sitting with his head in his knees. He was sobbing.

Kinga bent down and patted his shoulder. "You want to tell us what's going on?" she said kindly.

Oliver lifted his face to look at her. His eyes were red and puffy, and there was a snot bubble coming out of his nose.

"I didn't want to, but I didn't have any choice!"

"What do you mean?" Tyrone said.

"Max..." Oliver said, wiping his nose on his sleeve.

"The local kid from the seafront?" Jase asked.

Oliver nodded. Tears were running down his freckled cheeks. "I ... I thought we were friends. He let me ride on his electric scooter, but I crashed it. It was only a scratch, but Max lost it. Said that I owed him the cost of a new scooter. And that if I didn't get the money by Sunday, he was going to get his gang to beat me up. I didn't know what to do. We don't have that kind of money, and there was no way I could make it in a week. But then ... I found this."

He pulled a key out of his pocket.

"Mr Collins' skeleton key!" Jase said.

"Yeah. I've been using it to sneak into people's caravans and steal stuff to make the money."

Jase had known bullies like Max before. Back on his estate, there had been an older boy called Billy, who had terrorized the rest of the kids. Story was, Billy had broken a boy's nose just for looking at him funny. Everyone was scared of him. And he fed off their fear. The more scared they were, the more powerful Billy became, until he was untouchable. Untouchable, that was, until Nana Rose moved on to the estate.

She saw what was going on and had a quiet word with Billy and he never bothered anybody again. To this day, Jase didn't know what she'd said. He wished he knew because maybe he could use it now.

"Why didn't you tell anyone?" Harri said, sitting down next to Oliver on the damp floor. "I mean, I know why you didn't tell Mum – she'd have blown a fuse – but you could have told me or Dad."

"I couldn't," Oliver said, looking down at the space between his knees again. "I was too ashamed."

Jase thought he understood. There were times when he'd been too ashamed to tell people about things. But he'd always felt better when he did.

"You complete and utter numpty," Harri said.

"Harri, I don't think that's helping," Tyrone said.

"But he IS! If he'd come to us, we could have come up with a plan!"

Oliver looked at his sister. "What could you have done?"

"We could have found another way for you to get

the money that didn't involve stealing!" She punched him lightly on the arm.

"What kind of plan?" Jase asked.

"Well, I don't know, I haven't thought of it yet. But between us, we can do it."

"She's right!" Kinga said. "We came up with this plan to catch you. We can come up with a plan to save you!"

"You'd do that?" Oliver said. "For me?"

"Once a Castle Rock Crew," Tyrone said, reaching his hand out for Oliver, "always a Castle Rock Crew."

Oliver stood up and slapped Tyrone's hand. Instead of doing the handshake, Tyrone grabbed his hand and pulled him into a hug.

"Right," Kinga said. "How much money are we talking?"

Oliver rubbed his eyes on the sleeve of his hoodie. "Max said he paid three hundred quid."

"Hmmm," Kinga said. She started pacing back and forth, her ballet pumps making squishing sounds on the tiled floor.

Harri took the rucksack off Jase. "Here," she said, passing the trainers back to Tyrone.

He hugged them to his chest and kissed them. "It's OK, babies, you're home."

"You're weirder than Oliver," Harri said.

She handed Jase back his phone and then dug around inside for a pen.

"Right," she said, taking the cap off the felt tip. She wrote "HOW TO MAKE £300" in big writing on the tiled wall. With three question marks after it.

"Without breaking the law," Jase said.

Harri added this to the wall.

"In just two days," Oliver added.

Harri scribbled this down too. But in smaller writing as she was running out of space.

They all stared at the writing on the wall, trying to think of a brilliant plan.

"We could busk," Tyrone said.

"That's a great idea!" Kinga said. "Ed Sheeran used to make hundreds of pounds in a day busking."

"Can anyone sing?" Harri asked.

They shook their heads.

"Dance?"

"Only what I know from TikTok," Kinga said.

Maybe not busking then.

"We could paint our faces silver and stand still like robots?" Kinga suggested.

They considered this, but decided that it would take more time than they had to make the money.

"We could rob a bank?" Harri said. "We have the necessary skills."

"Without breaking the law!" Jase said, reminding her of what was written on the wall.

"Banks don't count!" Harri said. "They're banks! They can just print new money!"

Jase rolled his eyes. "Pretty sure the police would have something to say about that."

He felt bad for Oliver, but he wasn't about to become a bank robber for the boy! He wracked his brain. The only way he'd made money in the past was by helping out around the house and his mum would give him some pocket money. What if they did that, on a bigger scale?

"We could do chores around the site?" he said. "Ask Mr Collins if he wants fences painted, that kind of thing."

"You reckon he'd pay us three hundred pounds?" Tyrone said hopefully.

Jase thought about this. Mr Collins wasn't their biggest fan. "Probably not."

He sighed. They were getting nowhere. He chewed on the inside of his mouth trying to think of ways to earn hundreds of pounds in less than two days.

"Face it," Oliver said, "it can't be done. I just have to take the beating."

"We're not going to let that happen," Harri said. "We can persuade Dad to pack up tonight and just go home."

"And never come back to Castle Rock?" Oliver said.

Harri bit down hard on her bottom lip. "If that's what it takes, yes."

Jase knew how much she loved this place. She'd said it was her happy place. But she was willing to give it up to keep her brother safe.

Oliver hugged her and kissed the top of her head. "OK, I'll tell Dad."

"I guess we could always win it," Kinga said.

They turned to her.

"What do you mean?" Jase asked.

Was there a competition they could win? Jase had a flash of Kinga in a boxing ring, standing over a huge man, one gloved hand raised over her head in victory. He wouldn't put it past Kinga to be an expert in boxing.

"On the Fantasy Island arcades," she said, snapping him out of the boxing dream.

"We are pretty amazing," Tyrone said.

"Amazing enough to make three hundred pounds?" Oliver asked.

"Just watch us," Harri said.

CHAPTER THIRTY

Adrenaline bubbled in Jase's belly as they rode towards Fantasy Island the following day, Sherlock running alongside. They had a mission. Win three hundred pounds. Give back the stolen items. Save Oliver.

They locked their bikes up quickly and squeezed through the mass of people waiting to enter. As they weren't planning on going on any of the roller coasters (which Jase was sad about), they didn't need wristbands.

The Saturday market was crowded with shoppers browsing the row of booths. They ducked around people picking out new clothes or souvenirs. Squeezed past people buying sticks of rock. And Jase very narrowly avoided knocking over a stall of nose studs.

At last, they arrived at the arcades.

There was a NO DOGS ALLOWED sign on the door.

"You have to wait here, boy," Jase said to Sherlock. He tied Sherlock's lead to a lamp post and stepped inside.

The ringing sounds and flashing lights hit Jase like a wall.

"OK, focus, everyone," Harri said as they walked through the doors. "Only games that pay out prizes; we can't get distracted by the video games." Jase was pretty sure she was talking to herself here. "I'm talking alley rollers, coconut shies. Pushers, grabbers and spinning arms." She counted off the games on her fingers. "We split up to cover more ground. Go, go, go!"

The others split off and found machines almost instantly. Jase didn't know which way to go. Everything was too loud and too bright. And he only had a handful of coins in his sweaty hands.

And then he saw a game just ahead.

Sink it.

The rules were simple. You had to throw a ping-pong ball into cups marked with different points. If you made it to 100 points you won. But you only got five balls.

Jase smiled. He wasn't very good at video games. But he and his brothers had played a family version of ping-pong for years. They didn't have space in the flat for a ping-pong table. But when Mum brought home a big bag of the small white balls, they'd created their own game. They'd put rows of mugs and cups in the hallway, and you could only move forward by throwing a ball into one of the cups. Land a ball in the cup, remove the cup, take a step forward. The first to get to the end of the hall was the winner. They called it Hall Ball.

And Jase was the reigning champion.

He pushed ten of his coins into the machine and five ping-pong balls rolled out of the slot.

He picked up the first ball, blew on it for luck, and threw.

Plonk. It landed straight in the 25-points cup.

Only 75 more points to go.

With his second ball, he slotted it into the 10-points cup.

Three more balls to go.

He aimed for the 50-point cup with his third ball. It bounced off the rim and landed in the 15-point cup next to it.

He decided to play it a little safer and aimed for the 30-point cup with his fourth ball. It went straight in and ... bounced straight out again.

He was on his last ball and had 50 points still to make.

It's OK, he told himself. *You can do this.*

He closed his eyes and imagined he was at home in the flat with his brothers. The ringing and shouting of the machines became their voices, jeering and teasing.

He took a deep breath, opened his eyes, and threw the ball.

It clipped the edge of the 50-point cup. Then rolled around and around the edge, like water being sucked down a drain. He held his breath and wished with everything he had.

The ball tipped over the edge and into the cup.

He'd done it.

The machine exploded in bells and lights. *Winner!*

Winner! Winner! it shouted at him. And a strip of yellow paper tickets started spitting out of the machine. The tickets fell like a waterfall and made a pile on the floor.

People around him cheered and he felt hands slapping his shoulders. He pulled the last ticket from the machine and scooped them all up in his hands.

He heard a whooping from the other side of the arcade and ran over to see Harri as a cascade of prize tickets poured out of one of the pusher machines along with special prizes. Jase caught her eye and held up his armful of tickets. Harri tapped the side of the machine and winked. She must have used her thwack method.

Hey, no one had said anything about not cheating.

Oliver was working on the pusher machine next to his sister. Along with tickets, there were also several plastic eggs holding special prizes in the machine. As Jase watched, Oliver managed to tip one of the eggs over the edge. There was a ringing of money paying out.

Oliver retrieved the egg and twisted it open.

"Twenty quid!" he said, holding a token up!

They were getting there.

Jase found Kinga on the grabber machine. She was ignoring the fluffy toys and focusing her energy on the expensive items which they could trade in for more tickets.

Her focus was absolute as she directed the claw over the target objects. She tapped the joystick with tiny, tiny movements, to get the grabber exactly where she wanted it.

The grabber opened, dropped and BRUSHED the top of a watch before retracting.

"One more go," Kinga said through gritted teeth.

She made the smallest adjustment to her targeting. The grabber opened, dropped and this time it picked the watch up.

Jase and Kinga jumped up and down as the watch was dropped through the collection shoot.

"That's my second one!" Kinga said, holding up another prize.

That had to be another thirty pounds easy. Slowly but surely, they were getting there.

Jase went to find Tyrone to see how he was getting on. He grinned when he found him.

On the basketball game, of course!

He had a crowd of people around him who were chanting something. Jase couldn't make it out over the noise of the machines until he got closer.

They were counting.

"Twenty-five!" they shouted as a ball fell clear through the basket.

Tyrone pulled another ball out of the cage and rolled it in his hands. He reached up on his toes and...

"Twenty-six!" the crowd cheered.

As the ball rattled through the machine, bells rang and it spat out a strip of tickets. The strip was already pooling on the floor.

"What's the most it will pay out?" Jase heard a boy ask one of the arcade staff who was watching the excitement with a bored expression while chewing on a lollipop.

The staff member was in his late teens, early twenties maybe. He had black greasy hair and wore a polo shirt that was a few sizes too big. It had "Tony" written on it. Tony pulled the lollipop from his mouth with a wet POP. "Game stops at thirty. But no one has ever got that many."

"Twenty-seven!" the shout went up as Tyrone cleared another shot. Another strip of tickets spewed out.

"Twenty-eight! Twenty-nine! Thirty!"

More alarms and bells rang and the machine played a triumphant song. Tyrone had beaten the machine.

The tickets spat out so fast it sounded like a printer.

"And thank you very much!" Tyrone said, gathering them all up.

Jase ran and jumped on Tyrone's back.

"That was amazing!"

Tyrone looked down at the tickets Jase was holding. "Looks like you've been doing pretty well yourself!"

"OK, OK," Tony the arcade worker said. "Enough of you guys now. Out."

"What?" Tyrone said, outraged. "But why?"

"Because I say so. You're making everyone look bad."

"You mean we're making *you* look bad," Jase said.

Kinga, Harri and Oliver had come to see what was going on.

"And you lot can do one too." Tony pointed to the exit.

"I demand to see the manager," Kinga said.

Tony smiled a crooked smile. "I am the manager. Now get out before I call security."

Tony ignored their protests and shooed them out of the arcade. He slammed the door in their face and topped it off by sticking his tongue out at them.

Jase untied Sherlock and they walked away from the arcade.

"Well," Harri said, "how did we do?"

They gathered around a park bench and started counting their tickets.

"Three hundred and thirty-three pounds in tickets and two watches worth twenty pounds each," Tyrone said.

Harri whooped. "That's even more than we hoped!"

She and Kinga hugged and the boys high-fived.

319

Only Oliver didn't look delighted. "Only one problem," he said.

"What?" Harri said. "It's more than Max's scooter is worth."

"It's not in cash."

They looked down at the pile of tickets and watches. Would it be good enough for Max? Or would Oliver still be in danger?

CHAPTER THIRTY-ONE

They found Max on the pier, throwing stones at seagulls. A strong wind blew off the sea, knocking over deckchairs and upturning umbrellas. But Max's spiked hair remained unmoving.

The gang of kids he'd been with last time was reduced to just two boys and one girl. The girl nudged Max when she saw Jase and the others arrive.

Max didn't turn around. He looked at them over his shoulder and then looked back out at the sea. "Well, what have we here, Oliver? Brought your little sister and her little friends as backup? What are they going to do? Nerd me to death?"

Max's friends chuckled even though it wasn't very funny.

"I'm here to pay my debt, Max," Oliver said.

Max slowly turned to face Oliver. He stretched his arms across the railings and looked up at the sky. Grey clouds were gathering. It looked like it might rain for the first time all holiday.

"About time," he said.

Harri stepped forward. She held out a pink plastic bag. In it was all their winnings.

Max recoiled from the bag as if it contained something stinky. "What is that?"

"It's three hundred and seventy-three pounds' worth of arcade prizes. Way more than Oliver owed you."

"That wasn't what we agreed, Oliver. I said three hundred pounds. In cash." He rubbed his thumb and fingers together. "Or else." He smashed a fist into the palm of his hand.

Oliver shook his head. "It was only a scratch, Max. Come on."

Max laughed. "Yeah, well, I'm adding interest for

emotional damage." He looked to his friends. They were slow on the uptake but laughed when they saw Max staring at them.

"It seems to me," Tyrone said, "that we are at an impasse."

"A what?" Max said.

"A situation in which no progress is possible," Kinga translated.

Tyrone nodded. "And you, Max, have a choice to make. You can have Oliver here beaten up. But of course that would mean we'd have to get the police involved. And it wouldn't be the first time you've been in trouble with the law, would it, Max?"

Max glared at him. "You wouldn't."

"Oh, we would," Jase said. "In fact, my nana was a chief constable and she knows exactly how to make sure bullies like you get what they deserve."

Max smirked, trying to act like he didn't care, but Jase could tell by the way he kept flexing his fists that he was worried. He tried to act tough, but he was just a scared posh boy at heart.

"Or you could take the tickets and go and have the best time in the arcades. Seems like a simple choice to me," Tyrone said.

Max's face scrunched up as he tried to think about what he was going to do. It looked like hard work.

"How about," Max said, pushing away from the railings and stepping towards Tyrone, "I have Oliver beaten up AND take the tickets."

His hand darted out and grabbed hold of the handle of the pink bag Harri was carrying. He yanked it hard, almost pulling Harri off her feet.

There was a low, rumbling growling. It sounded like thunder in the distance. Or the vibrations of a truck over concrete. It was coming from Sherlock.

The dog had his lips pulled back and his teeth bared. His ears were flat against his head and his body was rigid. Jase had never seen him like this before.

Max tugged the bag one more time and Sherlock leaped.

There was a loud squealing as Sherlock grabbed hold of Max's back pocket with his teeth. Max spun around, trying to get Sherlock off him. But Sherlock wasn't letting go.

"Get him off me! Get him off me!" Max shouted.

"Down, boy," Jase said.

Sherlock obeyed his master's command and let Max go free. There was a scrap of blue material still in Sherlock's mouth.

Jase bit down on his lips to stop himself from laughing when he realized what it was. There was a big hole in the back of Max's jeans. Through it, everyone could see his underpants. They had cartoon dinosaurs on them.

Max's friends looked down. They started pointing and laughing. Max covered the missing patch with both hands.

"If you want to hurt my brother," Harri said, stepping up to Max, "you'll have to go through me."

"And me," Tyrone said, pointing to himself with his thumb.

Jase took a step forward too. He realized he was taller than Max. Maybe even stronger. He'd never

been in a fight before and hoped he never would, but standing there with his friends beside him, he didn't feel so afraid.

Max looked up at him and shrank away.

"And you'll have to go through me and my dog," Jase said.

Sherlock growled again.

"Oh, and one last thing," Kinga said. She pulled her phone out of the top pocket of her denim jacket. "I've caught everything on camera. I'm sure the police will be interested in this."

Max looked like he'd just got off a roller coaster. His skin was green, and it looked like his legs were too weak to hold him up.

"Well," Tyrone said, "what will it be?"

Max looked at all of them. "OK, OK," he said. "Give me the money."

"Good choice," Tyrone said.

Harri handed over the bag. Max grabbed it and ran away, trying to hide the hole in his jeans in one hand, while carrying the money in the other. His friends took a look at the Castle Rock Crew and made a good choice as well. They ran.

"I can't believe it's over," Oliver said. "I don't know how to thank you. All of you."

"By making sure you never do anything like this again," Harri said.

"Well, I can't promise I won't mess up. But I can promise that if I do, I know who I'll turn to."

He wrapped his arm around his little sister, and the crew meandered back to the caravan site. It was starting to drizzle. A classic British summer. But they didn't mind. They laughed and teased each other the whole way back.

"You know what?" Harri said, as they got close to the entrance. "We make pretty good detectives."

"We do, don't we?" Kinga agreed.

"Maybe we should make a habit of it?" Harri continued. "You know: keep on solving crimes. Maybe we can start a podcast!"

"Or maybe," Jase said, "we can just close this case first."

"But we have already!" Kinga said.

"Nearly," Jase said.

Just one more thing and then they could close the book on the case of the Castle Rock Thefts.

They had to give everything back.

They used Mr Collin's skeleton key to undo what had been done. When the residents were out, the crew snuck in.

They left Mr Handley's watch on his kitchen table, and slipped Miss Johal's twenty pounds under a teapot in her kitchen. Both were left with a note written by Oliver.

"I am very sorry. I know what I did was wrong and I have learned my lesson. I will never, ever steal again. I hope that you can forgive me and that you will feel safe here on Castle Rock."

"And of course, this is yours," Oliver said as they were strolling back to their caravans. He handed Kinga back her camera. "I'm really sorry, Jase. I spent the loose change I stole from your place on the arcade."

"That's OK," Jase said. "I got my birthday coin back from the pusher machine thanks to your sister."

Harri grinned. "I am amazing."

"You're not bad," Oliver said.

"Go on then. Where is my stuff?" Harri said.

"What stuff?" Oliver said, like he had no idea what Harri was getting at.

"Come off it, Oliver. Give me my Switch!"

"Oh, that!" He pulled the console out from behind his back and handed it over to his sister. She snatched it and punched him on the arm again.

"I guess that's it," Jase said. "Case closed."

"Another mystery solved by the Castle Rock Crew," Tyrone said. And he and Jase bumped fists.

CHAPTER THIRTY-TWO

It was Sunday – Jase's last night at Castle Rock – and Tyrone's family were throwing a party.

Apparently, it was something they did every year. There would be food and music and dancing, and everyone was invited. It was Jase and Tyrone's job to make sure no one was missed. They went around the site knocking on doors, telling everyone about the party. They even stopped by Bob's camper van.

They knocked and waited. It took Bob a while to open the door. When he did, he smiled.

"Bob! We caught the thief!" they chorused.

Bob blinked in confusion but grinned back. "Oh, that's nice."

Jase wasn't totally sure that Bob remembered. "It wasn't Beryl after all," he said.

"Though she *was* a jewellery thief!" Tyrone added. And they bombarded Bob with all the details of what had happened. He smiled and nodded along, seeming to enjoy the excitement.

They also told him about the party. He looked down at his clothes. "Oh, I think my party days are behind me."

"Please come," Tyrone said.

"Yes, please. I know my nana would like to meet you," said Jase.

"We'll see," Bob said.

Jase didn't think Bob was going to come, but he knew someone who might be able to change his mind.

"I think that's everyone," Tyrone said, looking at the scrap of paper they'd been ticking names off.

"I feel like we forgot someone," Jase said.

They thought for a moment.

"Beryl!" they said together.

They diverted towards Beryl's caravan. When they

knocked on the door, it swung open. The room inside was empty. Every book, every knick-knack was gone. The only thing left was a photo which had been left on the kitchen table. It was a black-and-white picture of Catherine as a young woman receiving a gold medal for gymnastics.

Jase turned it over to read an inscription on the back.

I never could resist shiny things.

"I wonder if we'll ever see her again?" Tyrone said.

Beryl/Catherine was a criminal and she'd escaped justice. Again. And yet, Jase was OK with that.

"Somehow, I don't think so," Jase said, slipping the photo into his pocket.

Jase went back to get ready for the party.

There was music playing in the caravan and his auntie and nana were in a cheerful mood.

"Well, if it isn't our little detective," Nicki said as Jase walked in.

She grabbed him and twisted him around in time to the music. Jase allowed himself to be spun across the room.

"Well, come on then," his nana said, patting the settee next to her. "I want to hear all about it! I've told you my stories, and now I want to hear yours!"

Jase sat down and took them through everything that had happened. How Oliver had stolen the things and why. How they'd won the money he needed and how they'd stood up to Max.

"And everything is returned?"

Jase nodded.

He wasn't sure what his nana would think. Would she say that Oliver should be arrested anyway?

She ruffled his hair. "You and your friends should be very proud."

Nicki put on another song and pulled Jase back on to his feet. "You looking forward to the party tonight?" she asked.

Jase was. Although there was one thing that would make it perfect.

"What's wrong?" Nicki said, reading his serious expression.

Jase told Nicki and his nana about Bob not coming to the party. They listened intently, nodding.

When he had finished, Nicki grabbed her jacket.

"Where are you going?" Jase asked.

"Oh, just calling on a gentleman!"

The party was starting before Nicki returned, so Jase helped his nana get ready. The two of them walked out, arm in arm, and strolled towards Tyrone's caravan, Sherlock padding along beside them.

As they passed Beryl's caravan, Jase told his nana about how she'd done a runner.

"Looks like Catherine 'The Cat' is on the run again," Jase said.

"Wait. Who?" his nana said, stopping in her tracks.

"Catherine Carter-Calthorpe. Beryl's real name. Actually, she said you two went way back."

His nana shook her head. Then started laughing. And laughing.

"What is it?" He was worried this was a new

symptom of the dementia.

"I can't believe I didn't recognize her!" she said at last, wiping tears away. "I headed up the task force assigned to catch her. And we almost did. I tracked her to a flat in Skegness ten years ago, but when we got there she'd vanished. The one criminal I never caught, and she was right under my nose all along!" She laughed at Jase's shocked expression. "Come on," she said, ruffling his hair. "We have a party to get to."

The music was already pumping and there was the most delicious smell of BBQ wafting on the air.

Harri and her family were already there. Harri's mum had dyed her hair a new colour – orange – and she was wearing a jumpsuit to match. Her mum was dancing with an embarrassed but happy-looking Oliver, while Guy and Harri's dad were sharing a joke.

Mrs McGinty was there, wearing her earrings. They glinted in the low sunlight. She was chatting with Mr Handley and Miss Johal. They were excitedly showing each other the notes they'd received.

Mr Collins stormed towards them, a bunch of

keys jangling on his belt. After they'd returned all the stolen things, they'd returned his skeleton key, sliding it under his door. He looked like he might be about to complain about the party, when a chicken drumstick was pushed into his hand by Tyrone's dad. He took a bite of it and a look of delight spread over his face. Tyrone's dad slapped Mr Collins on the back and turned the music up.

Kinga and her mum and dad arrived. Kinga has managed to persuade them to stay just long enough for the party. She was dressed in a blue tutu over a pair of leggings and big black boots. She waved at Jase, then started gesturing towards the tray of food her dad was carrying, dramatically shaking her head.

"What's she trying to say?" his nana asked.

"I think she's saying don't eat anything her dad offers you."

Tyrone was running back and forth, delivering food for everyone.

He sped past Jase holding a tray piled high with sticky ribs. Jase, Kinga and Nana Rose all grabbed one.

They were the best ribs Jase had ever eaten.

Jase looked around at the party. Everyone looked like they were having a brilliant time.

Kinga's and Tyrone's older sisters were trying to make a TikTok dance video, but they kept messing up and laughing.

Harri was on the ground with Femi. They were building a rocket out of a plastic bottle.

Mr Collins and Mrs McGinty were dancing some king of jig. Jase felt a bony elbow in his rib. His nana was nudging him. She pointed over his shoulder.

He turned to see Nicki arrive at last. She was next to a man, helping him walk. It took Jase a moment to realize it was Bob. His hair was clean and brushed and he'd had a shave.

"You came!" Jase said.

Nicki helped Bob into a seat. "Your aunt is very … persuasive."

She made a small bow. "And you're going to start listening to your doctors and arrange yourself a carer, aren't you, Bob?"

Bob gave a sheepish grin. "I'll try."

"I'm part of a dementia support group," Nana Rose said. "If you're ever in Nottingham, you should come. It's not as depressing as it sounds. We mostly sing and sit around gossiping!"

"That sounds fun," Bob said.

Jase was distracted by the sound of a small explosion. He turned to see Harri's rocket blasting off. It flew high into the air and came back down. Before it could land, Sherlock leaped up and snatched it out of the air. He ran away with it and Harri chased after him.

Femi jumped up and down, squealing. "Again. Again."

There was one last surprise. Jase felt hands cover his eyes. He knew those hands. He knew that smell. He turned around to see his mum.

She was wearing a long dress and she had a new haircut. She looked more relaxed and rested than he'd seen her in ages.

"I've missed you!" She scooped him up in a big hug and swung him around. She placed him back on the

ground and put a hand on his head. "Have you grown?"

Jase did feel taller somehow. Or maybe it was just his new trainers.

"Oi, squirt!" It was Will, his eldest brother. And with him, Mark and Ross. The whole family were back together.

"What's this we hear about you solving a crime?" Ross asked.

Jase told them every bit of the case, right from the beginning. They didn't say it, but Jase knew they were impressed.

The sun set and the party kept going. His nana and Bob sang while people danced. Jase's brothers seemed to be busy vying for the attention of Tyrone's sisters. Tyrone was roped into the TikTok video, and they finally got it right.

Jase had arrived at Castle Rock only nine days before, worried he was going to be bored. Instead, he'd ended up making three new best friends and having the biggest, most incredible adventure of his life.

As much as Jase was looking forward to getting back to his own bed, he was sad to be going home tomorrow. He'd miss being part of the Castle Rock Crew.

And then he remembered what Tyrone had said. *Once a crew member, always a crew member.*

He couldn't wait till the next time they all got together. Who knew what adventures lay ahead?

SPECIAL THANKS

Jonny, Mum, Dad, Jenny, Carl, Kai, Dexter, Katie.

My Crew, who I struck gold with and come first always. McReidOwens – never a dull moment!

My Welsh family, Carol, Matthew, Chris, Sian, Charlie and Alfie, big Cwtch to you all.

To my friends, Jo, Chella, Johnny, Louis, Nikki, Banshee, Shane, Penny, Collette, friendships so solid I know I'll never stop laughing and feeling the love with you lot.

To my 'Our Dementia Choir' family, you have taught me more than you'll ever know, you've given music a whole new meaning and shown the world how to live well with dementia. I'll never give up the fight.

My 'Line of Duty' crew, Jed, Martin and Adrian, I hope this book has your approval to the Letter of the law! The Letter!

Now I get some strange and wonderful requests in my inbox, but writing a children's book was definitely up there! I called my sister Jenny, we chatted on the phone and started talking through ideas, recalling our childhood memories and the importance of friendship. From that moment Jenny was an integral part of the process. Jen, I could write an entire book on thanking you, and give a million reasons as to why you are so important to this book and my life … but short on space, so I'll just say WOOF. (Sorry for annoying 'IN' joke, don't worry, it's not that funny!)

Kim Curran, I want to shout from the rooftops about just how grateful I am to you! Thank you for sharing your incredible talents with me. When I outlined this story, you got it straight away, the characters and world I hoped we could bring to every page, you did just that and more!

To Lauren, Eugenie, Kate, Pip, the team at Scholastic, thank you for your belief, hard work and backing in everything 'The Jase Files'!

Kids, I wasn't a strong reader when I was young; even now I'm not the most confident reader but here's what I've learnt: go at your own pace, one word at a time, one day at a time, do it your way and with style!

Vicky

Kim Curran is the author of six books for teenagers. In addition to her writing, she's a Patron of Reading and a Royal Literary Fund Fellow. She's always taking up new hobbies and so far has done everything from fencing and boxing to climbing and even spoon whittling, all to prepare her for the inevitable zombie apocalypse. She lives in West London with her husband and dog.

You can find Kim on
Twitter and Instagram @kimecurran.